Blessings as
you continue to walk
with Jesus.
You've raised beautiful
girls.

Balance, Busyness, and Not Doing It All

Balance, Busyness, and Not Doing It All

Finding Balance During the Busiest Years of Parenting

BRENDA L. YODER, MA

Cover Photograph and Design by SuEllen Yoder Photography and Black Anvil Media

ISBN-13: 9781511966757
ISBN-10: 1511966750

Acknowledgements

*W*riting a book just doesn't happen. Here are those I need to acknowledge.

First, my writing friends and mentors who affirmed I'm a writer before having something published: Amelia Rhodes, who first said, "You're a writer." To Amelia and Ingrid Lochamire, you've both encouraged me, believed in me, pushed me, and critiqued me. Thank you for being mentors and friends. To Nicole O'Dell, who believed in and affirmed the work. To Elizabeth, Bonnie, and Ingrid who helped with final proofing, and to my entire writing group. Thank you ladies.

Thanks to the "Balance, Busyness and Not Doing It All" group; Ingrid, Devonna, Linda, Heidi, Jamelle, Holly, Stacy and Marian. This book would have never materialized had you not come along side and helped me put the retreat together for women who need it. Because you shared your gifts, time, talents, and prayer, this is reaching far beyond our sold-out crowd. Thank you for your faithfulness and generosity to women and me.

To the MOPS group in Zionsville, Indiana, and Lynn Strueh—this originated with your questions about balancing life and busyness. I love working with you, and pray God continues to grow each one of you as mothers and women of God.

To Star Patterson who first saw God's redemption in my motherhood journey and who believed in it, and to Marian Byrnes, who has mentored me.

To Cindy Hartman who read through a draft and is a great encourager.

To SuEllen Yoder, for the beautiful design cover and artistic talent.

To my intercessory prayer team - Ingrid, Devonna, Stacy, Heidi, Linda, Marian, Cynthia, Jasmine, Lou Anne and Terri. Thank you for your prayers and support of the ministry God's called me to do.

To Terri Burnett, my friend and encourager.

To Naomi, Helen, Tami, Amy, Melisa—we've lived this book as we've raised our kids together. Thank you for being there in many moments of motherhood.

To my mom, Arlene Lazzaro, who modeled order and detail in managing a home while working. You've always supported me and you are my biggest cheerleader. Thank you.

To Lois Yoder, my first mother-in-law, now deceased, who modeled everything in this book. To Catherine Yoder, my second mother-in-law, who models beauty of a strong woman who loves God. I love both of you.

To my sons, Brett, Andrew, and Kent, who make me laugh, speak truth, and encourage me. I'm proud of you and who God is creating you to be. Thanks for giving me lots of stories to tell.

To my only daughter, Kaylee Jayne, of whom I am most proud. You are an example of a woman God intends for each of us to be—loving, strong, nurturing, and beautiful in spirit. Your heart is fully His, an example for all women, young and old. "I love you" can never express the fullness of my pride and joy in you.

To my husband, Ron, who has *always* supported what God has called me to do. You've encouraged every opportunity that has come my way. You're also an example that men can do things out of their comfort zone. Thanks for sweeping, helping with the dishes, and being a great dad who doesn't babysit. Thank you for the many outings you've given me with friends over the years, and your affirmation of this ministry. I love you.

To my ministry partners Krissy Nelson and Lara Marriott who are my heart-sisters in ministering to moms.

To the moms who asked for this book before it ever was. You asked for it, so here it is. Lindsay, Nicki and Ashley, this is for you.

And to all the moms who just need encouragement—this is for you, too.

All honor and glory to my Lord Jesus Christ. May He be glorified.

Brenda Lazzaro Yoder, June 2015

Table of Contents

Introduction

I remember waking up, dreaming of retirement. Not that I wanted to be sixty-five, but I wanted time, space, rest, and quiet. I needed moments to myself just to breathe, and to let my mind be at peace.

There was something inherently wrong to be thirty-nine and longing to fast forward twenty years, missing the most vital years of your life.

We were exhaustingly busy.

"We" included my husband of eighteen years and our four children. He was a part-time teacher and a dairy farmer. I was a full-time teacher of high school students. Our children included a high schooler, a middle schooler, an upper elementary student, and a first grader. As the mom and the "holds-it-all-together-person" of this group, I was physically, emotionally, and spiritually exhausted. I lived for *next*.

Next week when this one was over.

Next season when this child's sport was finished.

Next year when the kids were older.

Next school year when I had a different set of students.

Balancing incredible busyness, while longing for *next*, I was missing God's best in life, relationships, and intimacy with Him. I lacked adequate self-care and personal peace. When you live life striving for next, you miss the fullness of now.

That's where I found myself.

It didn't particularly matter that I was working full time. I had been a stay-at-home mom for over ten years before I went back to the classroom. I still struggled with balancing everything then, too. I felt I had to serve as much as I could because that's what moms are supposed to do, right?

In my motherhood journey, I've learned the quality of our lives don't hinge on working or not working outside the home. They rest in priorities, intentional living, and making choices for each stage of parenting.

The answer to my dreams of retirement came when I realized I only had one life to live, and I needed to make personal and lifestyle changes. It took risks, but it's been worth it. I'm still living that life, daily making decisions as I continue to raise children in a culture where busyness is god. From these experiences, I encourage women and moms to seek what's most important where you are.

Then live it.

This book evolved from a retreat I present for moms with simple questions:

> *"How do you balance it all?"*
> *"How do you manage being a wife, mother, spending time with Jesus, and doing everything else?"*
> *"How can you be the perfect Christian woman?"*

The retreat, "Balance, Busyness and Not Doing It All," presents real life answers to these questions. After attending the retreat, women emailed asking for a book they could share with friends. They were thankful they weren't alone as moms who struggle. They said the encouragement and practical tips were life changing.

So that's what this book entails; how to balance living in the *now*, how to practically, intrinsically, and intentionally manage busyness without doing it all. How to say "no" to what's not important, so you can say "yes" to what is.

It's a hands-on, interactive resource with personal and practical tools to apply to your life, relationships, family, and household.

Because God is personal, and He cares about you.

So join us. You'll be encouraged, challenged, and perhaps stretched. The principles aren't theoretical, they're real. I have lived, am living, and will continue to practice each one as I, like you, face busyness every day.

The book is laid out in three sections. The *foundation of life balance* is the first section. The second section deals with the practical "how to's" of really managing houschold, family, life, and faith. The third section discusses the most important message of balance, busyness, and not doing it all—how to make your relationship with Jesus an integral part of your life and that of your family. Don't skip the sections because they build on one another.

I'm a teacher, so I won't let you cheat by moving ahead. You'll miss something.

Get a pen or pencil handy. Begin right now by asking the Holy Spirit to supply all of your needs through this material according to His glorious riches in Christ Jesus (Philippians 4:19). Amen.

The Foundational Things

One

A Case of Stolen Identity

"I have called you by name: you are mine."
ISAIAH 43:1B NLT[1]

*H*ave you ever felt like you're walking a tightrope, trying to balance the craziness of being a mom in the twenty-first century? No matter where you go, people say how busy they are. It's the answer to the common question, "How are you?"

If you're reading this book, you're probably searching for ways to balance the stress of being busy. Together, we're going to cover a lot of things to help you balance your life as a woman and mom.

But before you find balance, you need to find something that's missing.

It's your identity.

Have you had a case of stolen identity? I have. As women, we get lost in seasons of life trying to find ourselves. Have you ever thought about the different identities you have? Your identity's not lost as much as it is stolen. I never realized how my identity was misplaced until I was

---

1 New Living Translation, biblegateway.com

in crisis, not knowing who I was or how to navigate life. God showed me how mistaken identity affects every area of life, including unbalanced priorities and behavior.

Here's my case of stolen identity:

I've been a stay-at-home mom, wondering if I'd ever get out of the house.

I've been a working mom, wondering if I'd ever have time at home.

I've been a milking mom, as a dairy farmer's wife, feeding calves with a baby slung on my back.

I'm a volunteer mom, having served on every committee in church, except the food committee, because…

I'm a napkin mom, supplying store-bought goods to classroom parties because I don't like to cook.

I've been a volleyball, baseball, track, cross-country, gymnastics, piano, cheerleader, soccer, choir, band, theater, 4-H, tennis, and basketball mom.

I've been a running mom. Now I'm tired, so I'm an out-of-shape mom.

I'm a gardening mom, because pulling weeds is cheaper than therapy.

I've been a teacher-mom, endlessly grading papers.

I've been a student-mom, going to graduate school with peers the age of my kids.

Now I'm a counselor-mom, giving my teens the excuse to say, "Don't counsel me, Mom."

I'm also a writing and speaking mom, making my kids say, "Don't talk about that, Mom!"

I've been an angry and reactionary mom.

Now I'm a redeemed mom.

Above all, like you, I'm a daughter of the Creator who formed me in the depths of the earth (Psalm 139:13). This is our identity as women. You are fearfully and wonderfully made, in His image, and He declares it good (Psalm 139:14).

Are you hoping this book will help you manage the various roles you fill? It will. But there's more to a balanced life than meal planning or a how-to-list. You won't learn how to add more hours to your day.

You'll learn how identity, expectations, and your relationship with God are crucial for managing life.

The principles you'll learn aren't textbook theories. They're things lived and practiced through a relationship with Jesus Christ. As I've learned self-acceptance, grace, and the power of God in daily circumstances, He's transformed my life and my perspective of womanhood from one that's others-centered, to one that's Christ-centered.

That's the key to a balanced life.

Will you join me in finding the identity God's given you, so your life and family are centered in His priorities? We'll focus on what's important, amidst the busyness and noise distracting you from His purpose. You'll find God's best for you, so you can manage life no matter your season of parenting.

Seasons

As I'm writing this, leaves are falling outside the picture window, letting me know another season is about to change. Every autumn, I'm tempted to miss its beauty because winter is coming. I don't like the cold, snow, and darkness of Midwest winters. But I can't despise autumn because it leads to winter. When I do this, I miss autumn's beauty and the joy of harvest on our family farm.

Life is similar. There are stages of parenting where you're busy planning for the next season, and you miss the beauty of the moment you're in. Can you relate? Your schedule is full of activities getting your kids to the next stage. You overlook the joy and magic of simple moments. You strive for the next season, missing life that's happening now.

Balancing life while raising kids must be intentional, because good things steal your energy, time, and identity. As you create better balance, you'll discover God's priorities won't steal or destroy your identity, health, or family. Instead, your life will be centered on your relationship with Jesus Christ. His Spirit will help you in everything, from the smallest details of managing a home, to the hardest decisions that might require change.

The Road To Acceptance

Throughout this book, I'll be honest about failures and struggles, what's worked and what hasn't. Being vulnerable isn't easy. The majority of my life, I've been afraid to share what's inside of me. While I've looked fine on the outside, I've been a mess on the inside.

Have you ever been a mess?

In that messiness, I've felt alone. But you and I are not alone. God sees us. He sees the good, the bad, and the ugly and still loves us. Did you know that?

I remember the first time I realized God loved me despite my faults. I was eight or nine and was grounded for something I'd done wrong. I sat in my bedroom on my Holly Hobbie bedspread, and opened my children's Bible. A bookmark fell out listing various scriptures for different feelings. Skimming the list, the word "guilty" caught my eye. I felt guilty for whatever I had done. I opened the Bible to Psalm 51. Within those pages, words described my feelings:

"Against you, and you only have I sinned and done what is evil in your sight" Psalm 51:4 (NIV).[2]

"Create in me a pure heart, O God" Psalm 51:10a (NIV).[3]

The Jesus I learned about in Sunday School became real that day. The words of sin, confession, and forgiveness made me understand God saw everything about me and still loved me.

About a year later, I accepted Jesus Christ as my personal Savior through baptism, accepting His death on the cross and resurrection from the dead as payment for my sins. I understood He lived in my heart and I would have eternal life with Him in heaven when I died.

I knew, with Him, I was okay.

Even though I had that relationship with Jesus, I didn't know about my complete value, worth, and identity in Him until I was older. During

---

2 New International Version, biblegateway.com
3 New International Version, biblegateway.com

childhood, when my identity was forming, I was confused about who I was and where I fit.

Have you ever felt that way?

The youngest in my family, my identity was being the baby. In elementary school, my identity was outsider, being a move-in to a small, homogenous community. As I approached adolescence, I was more self-conscious about my differences with those around me. My ethnic name stuck out. My hair was too big. My family was different.

I wasn't one of *them*. I despised those differences.

When I was in seventh grade, someone made a comment about my weight. I thought if I couldn't be accepted because of my name, family, or natural appearance, maybe if I was thin enough, then no one would reject me for that particular reason. By the winter of my eighth grade year, I had lost over twenty pounds. I was diagnosed with anorexia nervosa when the disorder was just being identified.

At that time, interventions for eating disorders didn't deal with emotional issues, or faulty thinking about food or body image. While I tried to eat more, I didn't know how to emotionally or mentally handle the weight gain. I became bulimic, and remained bulimic until my early twenties after I had a child of my own.

While this story isn't connected to balance and busyness, what I learned about identity in Christ from overcoming an eating disorder is essential to my identity as a woman and mother. Similarly, your hurts and insecurities affect your identity as a woman and mom. Much of what we'll talk about in finding balance is grounded in identity and accepting yourself as is.

Do you need to accept yourself as is?

Accepting myself didn't happen immediately. It came after years of trying to be accepted by others. I strived to fit the image of what a good Christian wife and mom should be. I lived a life of *doing*, without learning to *be* as God created me. I was busy with good things, honestly believing my performance made me acceptable to others and God.

I tried to do it all.

But striving for perfection brought no peace. I felt like I was walking a tight rope, trying to balance everything. When life's storms came through extreme busyness, stress, and conflict, I crashed onto the waves below. My emotions were out of control. I realized something had to change, because it was damaging my family.

My Angry Mom Story

When I fell from the tight-rope of craziness, I was working full time, teaching 180 high schoolers, while raising four kids from kindergarten to high school. I was a wife and active church leader. I was also exhausted. Day after day, I woke up longing for peace and rest. I felt trapped by busyness, and there was no end in sight.

I was only forty.

For the first decade of parenting, I was a stay-at-home mom before going back to work as a high school teacher. After several years of teaching, my work load grew as class sizes swelled, and my own children grew up. Mental and emotional stress turned into irritation, anger, and frustration with my own kids. Our family was filled with conflict.

My husband, also a teacher, kept telling me each school year would get easier. One summer, I told him, "When it gets easier, the children will be gone. I can't handle this." I also knew the conflict in our home couldn't continue. Being stressed and emotionally exhausted, I knew if something didn't change, my children would remember me as an angry, contentious woman.

That's every mom's dream.

I needed to change my behavior. I needed to alter the source of my stress, exhaustion, and busyness. Taking a financial, professional, and personal risk, I packed up my classroom at the end of that school year and said good-bye to a profession I love.

It was the hardest decision I've ever made.

But it was worth it. I now work in a different profession with less stress and more work options. Reclaiming personal wholeness and balance in our family didn't happen overnight. A relationship with Christ provided the necessary strength.

The Foundation

Balancing life and priorities takes commitment, courage, and hard work. Accepting your God-gifted identity requires honesty with yourself, and God. It demands courage to shut out what others say about you or your decisions. It requires placing you and your children in God's hands, trusting Him for outcomes when you live in obedience.

Joel 2:25-27 says, *"I will repay you for the years the locusts have eaten— the great locust and the young locust, the other locusts and the locust swarm— my great army that I sent among you. You will have plenty to eat, until you are full, and you will praise the name of the Lord your God, who has worked wonders for you; never again will my people be shamed. Then you will know that I am in Israel, that I am the Lord your God, and that there is no other; never again will my people be shamed"* (NIV).[4]

This passage describes how God redeems years filled with regret. It's His promise that today is never too late to change priorities. It's about embracing His hope and receiving His truth no matter what you wish you could redo. It's confessing sin, receiving His forgiveness, knowing you'll never be shamed again.

I've seen Jesus Christ do this in my life and that of my family. I walk in that promise, daily. I've learned life isn't about meeting the expectations of others, only God's. It doesn't matter whether you work outside or in the home, being a godly woman is about an intimate relationship with Him, lived out in relationship with others, and fulfilling the unique call He's given you.

If you've experienced regret over things you wish you'd done differently, confess it to God. Receive His grace and forgiveness, and walk forward. While God doesn't give us back time, He redeems the time we have.

---

4 New International Version, biblegateway.com

I'm walking forward with you. With two adult children and two teen-agers, I'm still parenting, working, managing home and marriage, too.

How will you and I do it all?

By doing what's essential; finding our identity in Christ and allow-ing Him to prioritize what's most important now.

Will you join me?

Reflection

The following scriptures focus on your identity in Christ. Write down what you learn from each passage.

John 1:12

John 15:15

Romans 15:7

Genesis 1:27

I Corinthians 12:27

Galatians 3:27-28

I John 3:1-2

Colossians 3:1-3

Colossians 3:12

Psalm 139

Ephesians 1:4-5

Ephesians 1:11-15

Ephesians 2:10

Which verses are meaningful to you?

Which verses clarify your identity?

Father, thank you for being the Redeemer of people, time, and relationships. Thank you for being with me in every moment of my life. Thank you for bringing me to this moment where I can stop, breathe, and rest in You. Teach me what you want me to learn in each chapter so I can fully rest in You. Amen.

Two

FIRST, YOU'RE A WOMAN

*"So God created mankind in His image. In the
image of God He created him; male and female
He created them. God blessed them…"*[5]

GENESIS 1:27, 28A, NIV

Before you were a mom, you were a woman. Understanding this distinction is the first step in finding your identity. Do you consider being a woman first before you think of yourself as a mom?

When God created the first woman, He created her to birth life that would glorify Him. He created her to be a reflection of Him, to have communion and relationship with Him. He made her to be an extension of Him, His Son, and His Holy Spirit.

God gave woman His nurturing qualities. She is a life-giver, drawing others to Him, bringing tenderness, compassion, and truth into the world.

God created woman fully good, in His image, representing His character for His honor and glory.

---

5 New International Version, biblegateway.com

"Everyone who is called by my name, whom I created *for my glory*, whom I formed and made." Isaiah 43:7, NIV[6]

When God created you, He also made you in His image, for His honor and glory. He made you with the same qualities as Eve. He made you as a woman, first, before any other role you have. He created you as an extension of Himself.

You are His daughter, a reflection of His goodness. Do you know that?

Will you believe that?

God has a plan and a purpose for your life. Being a mom is just part of the plan.

There's a lie the enemy has been telling moms. He's been telling you being a mom is your sole identity. It's not true. Being a mom is only a part of who you are.

It's a role you fill; it's not your identity.

I want you to read that again.

Being a mom is a role you fill; it's not your identity.

When I first learned this concept, it took a while for it to sink in. Ever since I was a little girl, I dreamed of being a mom. I spent hours as a child playing house and Barbies, dreaming of my own family I'd have someday. Did you? My life's compass as a teen and young adult pointed towards being a mom.

I thought when I became a mother, my destiny would be complete.

As a girl, you're told your value and worth as a woman is tied to being a mother. It's a powerful lie. It gives the perception that single or married women without children are incomplete. It makes mothers misplace their value. When you base your worth on your child's performance or how others think you're doing as a parent, your worth is conditional. I don't how many times "bad mom" has rolled around in my head when I've failed as a parent or when my kid's actions are embarrassing, hurtful, or their choices are not-so-wise.

If these things defined me, I would be doomed. So would you.

---

6 New International Version, biblegateway.com

Instead, your worth is *unconditional* in God's eyes.

The roles you fill don't define you. Your place and value as God's daughter in His kingdom defines you. You are a woman, first, then a wife, mother, daughter, friend, or employee. As you begin to claim your identity in Christ and embrace His calling for you as a woman, you'll be able to put your role and responsibilities as a mom into perspective.

Being mom doesn't make you arrive in life.

Just being a woman is enough.

You're first a daughter of the King, assigned to bear and nurture life, like Eve. This is your identity. Defining your worth by your mom-performance will inevitably label you either as a "good mom" or a "bad mom." When I was a stay-at-home mother, I thought not working outside the home made me a "good" mom. When God called me to work in public schools, it contradicted what I thought a Christian mom should do. My identity was shaken. When I asked God to show me what it meant to be a godly woman, He told me it was being obedient to Him, no matter where I was. That was the first time I realized my identity was not based on my parenting role or profession, but on my position as His daughter.

When your identity is centered on motherhood, it'll be shattered when your kids screw up. If what others think becomes your guiding force for your identity, you'll hear accusations saying you're a "bad mom." Your children will fail you and you'll fail your children. It doesn't mean you're a failure.

It's natural to respond to your child's negative or embarrassing choices with fear of judgment. This is exactly where the enemy wants you to dwell. If he can keep your identity grounded in circumstantial successes or failures, then you'll never be sure of who you are.

You'll also never be sure of who God is.

Your identity as a woman isn't in your performance or that of your kids. Your calling is to nurture and give life, representing these aspects of God's character.

Women are life-givers.

Women without children also are life-bearers, giving life to others through encouragement, care, and nurture. Their value isn't any different than yours. If you're a mom, God has birthed life through you by having children. He's given you additional tasks of nurturing children under your care, whether those kids are by birth, adoption, fostering, or step-families. When you focus on equipping kids to be a reflection of God's character, images of being a "good mom" fade in comparison to the confidence you have fulfilling your calling as a life-bearer reflecting Christ.

What you believe about your identity is crucial in understanding how to balance life, expectations, parenting, and the demands of others.

You're a woman, first.

You're designed to give life to others through nurture, truth, compassion, and encouragement for the honor and glory of God. As you reflect His character and rest in His identity, a peaceful balance engulfs your soul.

Being a mom is what you do. It's not who you are.

Will you receive that?

Reflection

What roles are you currently holding that distract you from defining yourself as the daughter of the Most High God? List all of the roles you fill right now. (Example: wife, daughter, etc.).

Will you release them to God, asking Him to show you who you are in Him?

Dear Father, thank you for creating me in your image to nurture, provide life, compassion, strength, and truth. Help me to dismiss the lies telling me my identity is in the roles I fill, not in who I am in you. Teach me, Father, to have my identity grounded in you. Amen.

Three

You're Born to Be, Not Do

"You are precious and honored in my sight."
Isaiah 43:4 NIV[7]

$\mathcal{L}$et's apply these identity principles. What about your case of stolen identity? Have you thought about the various roles you have? If you haven't yet, take a moment to identify and write down all the roles you fill:

It's one thing to list those roles, but it's another thing to separate them from your identity.

---

7 New International Version, biblegateway.com

Remember, you're a *life-giver*.

The roles you fill are something you *do*. They aren't who you are.

Your worth isn't dependent upon on what you do. It's not found in titles, or things you accomplish. You're complete just how God made you. Though He created you as a life-giver, He also created you with a specific personality, temperament, gifts, and skill set. He created you to *be* who you are!

Because we each have distinct personalities, nurturing looks different. If you think, "I'm not good at nurturing," be encouraged. God has specific ways for you to nurture each of your kids that's personal. Ask Him to show you.

He will.

He's created you to nurture your kids perfectly. It's taken me years to really understand, believe, and receive this truth.

Is it hard to believe you're okay the way you are? We're raised to perform. There's a lie that if you do more, do better, or look prettier, you're acceptable. Like me, most girls start believing this lie as a young teen. However, when you become a mom, the pressure to perform multiplies. The mom-lie says if you volunteer more, have a cleaner house, a better body, and well-behaved kids, you're acceptable and worthy. Have you believed that lie?

These things don't increase your value in God's eyes. He loves and accepts you, just the way you are.

Doing *more* doesn't make you the person He created you to be.

When you strive for more to feel good about yourself, or meet someone's expectations, you're busy with unnecessary things for wrong reasons. Accepting who you are, and being comfortable with yourself should shape your priorities. When it does, you release the picture-perfect image.

You are enough the way you are.

Who's that ideal woman you're striving after? The one whose Pinterest boards are filled with success and whose children sit perfectly still? The Proverbs 31 woman?

A wife of noble character who can find?
She is worth far more than rubies.
Her husband has full confidence in her
    and lacks nothing of value.
She brings him good, not harm,
all the days of her life.
She selects wool and flax
    and works with eager hands.
She is like the merchant ships,
    bringing her food from afar.
She gets up while it is still night;
    she provides food for her family
    and portions for her female servants.
She considers a field and buys it;
    out of her earnings she plants a vineyard.
She sets about her work vigorously;
    her arms are strong for her tasks
She sees that her trading is profitable,
    and her lamp does not go out at night.
In her hand she holds the distaff
    and grasps the spindle with her fingers.
She opens her arms to the poor
    and extends her hands to the needy.
When it snows, she has no fear for her household;
    for all of them are clothed in scarlet.
She makes coverings for her bed;
    she is clothed in fine linen and purple.
Her husband is respected at the city gate,
    where he takes his seat among the elders of the land.
She makes linen garments and sells them,
    and supplies the merchants with sashes.
She is clothed with strength and dignity;
    she can laugh at the days to come.

She speaks with wisdom,
    and faithful instruction is on her tongue.
She watches over the affairs of her household
    and does not eat the bread of idleness.
Her children arise and call her blessed;
    her husband also, and he praises her:
"Many women do noble things,
    but you surpass them all."
Charm is deceptive, and beauty is fleeting;
    but a woman who fears the Lord is to be praised.
Honor her for all that her hands have done,
    and let her works bring her praise at the city gate.
                    Proverbs 31:10-31 (NIV)[8]

Neither Pinterest, nor Proverbs 31:10-31, are a fair representation of a woman's daily life. The woman described in Proverbs 31 isn't a snapshot of a woman doing all of those things at one point in time. She's a woman displaying godly characteristics over a lifetime.

I bet her kids didn't rise up and call her blessed when she grounded them.

God doesn't condemn you when you miss the Proverbs 31 standard. Like any other biblical admonition, the Holy Spirit does the work when we release ourselves to Him.

What You'll Lose

In the Western cultures, working equals worth, which equals worthiness. The idea that your worth is defined by doing something is a cultural principle, not a biblical one. It's another lie that motivates your busyness and out-of-balanced priorities. The unofficial mom-rule is that the woman who does it all is the best. She's the one who has everything together, who can handle it all.

---

8 New International Version, biblegateway.com

Her name is Superwoman, and she doesn't exist.

If you try to be her, you'll lose yourself.

If you think you've already lost yourself, you're not the first mom who's thought that way. Remember the roles I thought shaped my identity? I truly believed the more productive I was, the more acceptable I was. Do you believe that, too? Have you ever wondered who you are inside of that Supermom cape?

By letting the Supermom image go, you open yourself up for the fullness of who God created you to be. So stop striving for more, and rest in how He's created you. Ask God how you can use your gifts and talents to bless your family and others around you.

You were born to *be*, not do.

Your heavenly Father wants you to accept the beauty of who you are in Him. He wants you to develop the priorities He has for you as His daughter, first. Those priorities will shape you to be the wife or mother He's called you to be.

He wants you to seek Him, to be still, knowing He is the Lord who equips you for the tasks He's given you. He wants you to know you are more than what you do.

You are enough being who you are.

The Price of Doing It All

It's dangerous when women try to be Supermom. Not only do you lose yourself trying, but it's costly to your mental and emotional well-being, no matter if you work inside or outside of the home. When I was a stay-at-home mom trying to do it all, I was stretched emotionally and physically. As a full-time teacher, I was pulled in different ways. I prepared lessons, graded papers for 180 students, parented four active kids, and served in church and community. While my classroom and household ran smoothly, I was constantly stressed and irritable with our hectic life.

Are you ever stressed and irritable?

Doing it all carried a high price for my family and my emotional well-being. For me, leaving a high-stressed profession for mental, emotional, and physical rest was the best choice at the time. If you find yourself feeling similarly stressed and exhausted, consider the cost that doing it all is having on your health, and that of your family.

In trading the do-it-all lifestyle for a better balance of work, family, and home, this is what I've learned:

Doing it all is pricey. Though our family functioned well on the surface, I was emotionally fragile. I took my frustration, irritation, and stress out on my kids. My behavior almost destroyed our family. Walking a tight-rope lifestyle isn't healthy.

Decisions about lifestyle changes are hard. When I switched careers, I was heart-broken. I love teaching. Leaving a stable career to go back to school full-time was also financially risky. But those decisions have blessed our family, and provided peace of mind. They've allowed me to trust God in new ways.

Perseverance pays off. Going back to college in mid-life wasn't easy. I was scared and out of my comfort zone. There were no guarantees. But persevering paid off. God's provided a job that fits our family life. He's brought emotional and spiritual healing. He's been faithful. He can do the same for you.

Self-awareness is important. Knowing yourself, and your limits, is crucial for a balanced life. Being okay with those limits is even more important. I've learned what I can and can't handle, and feel comfortable saying no to things. As you understand your limits and how they relate to priorities, you'll find balance, too. (We'll learn more about these principles in later chapters.)

As a mom, you're the first example your children have of women. Raising three sons makes me aware of a man's understanding and expectations of women. Do we teach them women have value outside of their roles of mother, and wife? When we strive to do it all, do we model the picture society has of women, or the one God has?

What about you? Will you let go of the Supermom image? Will you be still and hear God say:

You are mine. And that's enough.

⟶

Reflection
What lies have you been told about performance and acceptance?

What are *your* unique gifts and characteristics? List the things you enjoy doing that make you feel alive.

What current situations make you stressed or irritable? Write them down. Place them at the feet of Jesus.

What activities are you doing that draw time and energy away from being who God's created you to be?

What activities or responsibilities is God prompting you to eliminate or decrease for this parenting season?

Father, thank you for accepting me completely for who I am. Equip me to do the same. Help me to stop performing, and striving for more. Allow me to just be me. Amen.

Four

LETTING GO OF THE HIGH WIRE ACT

*Busyness isn't the answer to balancing
life. Prioritizing your time is.*

Remember that high-wire act we've talked about? On a scale of one to ten, how would you rate yourself on the intensity of juggling all of your roles? Are you on the low-end, fairly stress-free with the responsibilities you have? Are you a well-balanced five, finding equilibrium with your various duties? Or are you a frazzled ten, just waiting for your demise? Rate yourself on the scale below:

1   2   3   4   5   6   7   8   9   10

(Calm/balanced)   (teetering but ok)   (About to crash)

Being a mom shouldn't be a high-wire act. Do you think God intends your energy to be spent frantically balancing things, wondering when you'll fall apart? When your time is spent orchestrating craziness, there's not stamina left for what's important. You're also not prepared for life's storms that knock you off balance.

Like tight-rope walkers, you need a strong core for proper balance. Stabilizing your emotional, mental, and spiritual core includes letting go of what's unimportant, so you can hold onto what is. Strengthening your inner-being equips you to fulfill your calling as a woman, wife, and mom.

Above activities or performance, kids long for *you* before anything else. They want the security, love, and closeness you give them. When you're comfortable with yourself, personalizing how you nurture your child, you both flourish in intimacy with each other.

Were you tense and nervous when you first breastfed your babies? Your newborn may have cried because he sensed your insecurities. When you became comfortable with the process, your little one was more relaxed, too.

If you didn't nurse, your baby still thrived as you nurtured in other ways. Once you let go of the breastfeeding expectation, you probably thrived, too.

Other aspects of parenting are similar. When you're comfortable with your natural abilities, you can release expectations. You're more relaxed in your roles. You don't criticize yourself for not living up to the ideal image of motherhood. Your confidence increases. Insecurities diminish. You embrace your gifts, using them to nurture your children.

What's Most Important

As a daughter of the King, it's important to have the right perspective on your royal duties. Your divine job is life-giver, not performing, or being busy. Serving on another committee or helping out *one more time* doesn't benefit your child. When I understood a mom's primary role as a life-giver and nurturer, my perspective on priorities changed. Since then, it shapes my decisions, time, and energy. It takes the focus away from doing *more*.

Personalizing how you nurture is crucial. Did you know God uniquely created you for your family? The way you nurture should reflect your gifts and strengths. That's God's unique design for your family. It's unlike any other. For me, nurturing includes one-on-one times with kids, reading books at bedtime, listening to and saying prayers with them. It involves delegating responsibilities, so I have more time to play and engage with them.

The way you nurture may look different. And that's okay.

When priorities are centered on your kid's intrinsic needs, it appropriately guides your time and energy. It takes the focus away from juggling life, bringing peace and perspective to a healthy equilibrium.

Do you need that?

The Importance Of Nurture

When you watch mothers in the animal kingdom, their natural instinct is to care for their young; to protect and nurture them. But nurturing doesn't come naturally for everyone. When you personalize it, making it specific to you and your kids, you release the condemnation of unwritten mom-rules saying you have to do it a certain way.

According to Merriam Webster online dictionary, nurture is helping something or someone to grow, develop or succeed.[9] God wants you to grow your children; to develop them according to His plan and design. This looks different for each child, for each stage, and for each mother-child relationship.

There's a stereotype that a nurturing mom is sweet and cuddly and has home-made meals on the table each night. That's not accurate. Stop trying to be her. Instead, create an environment for you and your children based on your individual temperaments. One child may love being held and another one doesn't. For each child, find what makes them feel like you *know* them.

That's what nurture looks like.

Those of us currently raising kids have an additional assignment as nurturing parents in an information driven society. Families are increasingly disconnected and disenfranchised, even in Christian homes.

---

9 merriam-webster.com/nurture

Technology, smartphones, and social media make relationships more superficial and less engaging. Kids are highly sexualized, desensitized to violence, disconnected, and lonely. Even in well-meaning homes, kids easily can be isolated and disconnected from interpersonal relationships. Because of this, nurturing is even more important for kids in a disenfranchised society.

An experiment by Harry Harlow in 1966 exemplifies the basic effects of nurture. Monkeys were put in controlled environments with fake mothers. One "mother" was made of chicken wire and the other was made of cloth. The monkeys preferred the "mother" made of cloth to the one made of chicken wire, even when a feeding bottle was placed with the mother made of chicken wire.

Even when the monkeys were hungry, they preferred the "mother" who was softer and warmer.[10]

Kids are the same way. Softer and warmer means being available when kids need you. It means listening to them, and encouraging them to reach their full potential. When you nurture your kids instead of being occupied with busyness, it impacts your kids.

Though the nature versus nurture debate is routinely tested, there's ample research concluding lack of nurture during a child's development contributes to certain mental health problems and personality disorders.[11] Because of an increasingly disconnected society, children who are given security, love, and nurture will impact those around them.

The time you invest nurturing your child is a kingdom investment, not just a personal one.

Arbitrary busyness isn't a substitute for God's best. It distracts from what's important. It impacts God's will for yourself and your family in this generation. Consider tasks which pull you in all directions, taking significant time away from your family and kingdom investments.

Is that God's best for you?

---

10 The Science of Love: Harry Harlow & the Nature of Affection. http://psychology.about.com/od/historyofpsychology/p/harlow_love.htm

11 World Health Report 2001, Mental Health:New Understanding, New Hope. World Health Organization:2001

What You Can Control

Do you feel like life is controlling you, keeping you on that tight rope? It doesn't have to. You hold the keys to your stress levels, priorities, and the amount of busyness you're living. Is that a new concept for you?

I used to believe my life was controlled by the status quo—work, kids' activities, and expectations of others. I felt bound by circumstances. When stress levels and emotions were out of control, I started focusing on things I could control instead of blaming the circumstances.

As I made adjustments, things began to change. I *did* have control over life's craziness.

You can, too.

Responsibilities, priorities, and quality of life are three things you control that positively or negatively affect your life, and that of your family. It doesn't matter what stage of parenting you're in, you can change these areas if they're out of balance. (You'll get practical tips on how to do this in upcoming chapters).

For some of you, what you control may be complicated because of toxic people, relationships, or extenuating circumstances in your marriage or family. In these situations, it's important to focus on the things you *can* control—expectations, health, attitude, and thoughts. Solutions for complicated situations can't be addressed in a few short paragraphs. When circumstances are complicated, though, you still control your responses, and your quality of life.

When I felt bound by the behavior of others, I realized I couldn't control their behavior, only my responses. I couldn't blame them. I could only blame myself for how I let their actions drive my reactions and stress. As my responses changed, I gained power and freedom over myself and the situation.

Do you feel chained to your season of life, unrealized dreams, or demanding relationships? Are you bound by fear of what would happen if you stopped blaming others? There's freedom when you focus on what you control rather than what you can't change. Instead of walking a tight rope, you'll feel like you can fly.

Busyness, circumstances, and others don't have to control you. You have control over your life.

My wake up call for change was realizing I wasn't the mom I wanted to be. I was a stressed, busy, irritated, and angry woman.

As you consider your priorities, and what you have control of, ask yourself what I did:

If you were to die today, how would your children remember you?

Let the answer define your expectations, choices, and priorities.

⁓

Reflection

God created you for your family. Answer the following questions to make nurture personal to you and your family:

What expectations about nurture do you need to let go?

How can you personalize nurturing for you and your family?

What do you blame for your busyness, stress, or unhealthy responses?

What's within your control that *you* can change for better quality of life?

⟋

Lord, thank you that change is never out of my reach. Help me change what I can, and prioritize what is important. Through the upcoming chapters, teach me how to define my priorities, having courage to change what's needed. Thank you for equipping me in all things. Amen.

Five

FINDING STRENGTHS AND ACCEPTING WEAKNESSES

*But He said to me, "My grace is sufficient for
you, for my power is made perfect in weakness,
for when I am weak, I am strong."*

2 CORINTHIANS 12:9 NIV[12]

How your children perceive you is important, but even more important is what you think of yourself. The next few chapters are the heart of creating balance because they include how to balance yourself, your strengths and weaknesses, and embracing them both.

Priorities are often motived by self-perception. Changing what you control begins with accepting who you are—the good, the bad, and the ugly. Do you accept everything about you? God does. Being comfortable with yourself frees you up to be a better nurturer. It also releases you from the bondage of life's craziness.

Five easy steps won't create balance. Accepting who you are will.

---

12 New International Version, biblegateway.com

My Defining Moment

I laid on our couch, sobbing. It was a Sunday afternoon. I was reeling from a comment someone made that morning. I loathed myself, again. Why did I always mess up? I was mad at God for making me the way He did.

Why couldn't I just be normal?

I heard a quiet voice. "I made everything about you. I made you with those weaknesses. There's not one thing about you I overlooked. I love you the way you are. Your weaknesses are where I work best. When you despise yourself, you despise Me," He said.

God's words flooded my soul. As a young mom, it was the first time I realized my weaknesses were His design. They weren't my fault. They weren't to be despised.

They weren't mine to loathe. My weaknesses belonged to Him.

God has shown me when you accept yourself as He created you, surrendering to Him, He pours Himself into your weaknesses.

Have you ever loathed yourself? Have you looked at your failures and weaknesses, and felt completely worthless? When you look at other women, do you try to be like them, only to find yourself bankrupt in comparison?

I have. I've spent most of my teen and adult years hating myself and my weaknesses. I've tried to live up to others' expectations, only to feel like a failure. The crying-on-the-couch moment was the first time God's truth broke through the lies I believed about who I was. And who He is. I finally understood He loves all of me.

He loves all of you, too.

God's Truth

Psalm 139 says God knew you before you were even born.

"My frame was not hidden from you when I was made in the secret place, when I was woven together in the depths of the earth. Your eyes saw my

unformed body; all the days ordained for me were written in your book before one of them came to be" Psalm 139: 15-16, (NIV).[13]

Your Creator knows everything about you. There's nothing about you that's hidden from Him. If you believe His Word is true, then you can believe He made the sum of who you are, including your strengths and weaknesses. He desires to use both for His glory.

Did you know God can be glorified in your weaknesses, when you allow Him to work in those areas?

A term I heard from Pastor Kenn Gividend in his book, *The Prayer of Hannah*, further changed my perspective about weaknesses. Instead of using the discouraging term of weaknesses, he refers to them as *lesser-strengths*.

I like that, don't you? The term lesser-strengths reframes what you believe about the areas in which you struggle. It changes something negative to something God can empower and change. Instead of perceiving weakness as a defeating failure, you define it as a lesser-strength God can use for His glory.

For years, I knew a lesser-strength of mine was words. I misused words by reacting in anger, or speaking in absolutes to get my point across. The little girl who spoke explosively to be understood became an adult. Uncontrolled words hurt people I love.

When I began surrendering words and emotions to God, He began using them for His honor and glory. He's covered my weakness with His power, bringing healing and hope to others. When you strive in your lesser-strengths without surrendering them to Him, He can't work. It brings more angst to an unbalanced life.

But surrendering your shortcomings isn't the only step in creating balance. Many of us not only strive in our weaknesses, but try to live in another person's strengths. Being busy with things because other people do them makes your efforts, priorities, and energy out of balance.

---

13 New International Version, biblegateway.com

Do you compare yourself, putting yourself down because you can't do what other moms do? Do you try to be someone else, instead of who God has created you to be? When you emulate the strengths of others, you lack God's power because another person's gift isn't what God wants to use in you.

In addition to comparing yourself to other women, do you try to meet expectations from the culture, media, church, or other people? These aren't God's expectations. They distract you from what God says about you.

You're an imperfect person. Stop trying to fix yourself. God only created one perfect person, His Son, Jesus Christ. He made you beautiful the way you are.

Accepting and releasing your lesser-strengths allows God to glorify Himself through them. His grace meets your weaknesses, and manifests His power and majesty where you can't.

Believing this truth is essential for a balanced life.

Accept what you can't change. Embrace what you can. Acknowledge that your weaknesses aren't your fault, and that God can use them. Establish realistic expectations that bring strength and joy rather than heartache and frustration.

Defining Your Strengths. Letting Go of the Lesser Ones

Understanding God's plan for weakness is a first step in gaining balance. The second step is defining your strengths and lesser-strengths so you can utilize the gifts God's given you.

Each of us has different strengths. What are the areas in which you excel? What gives you joy and energy? Identifying your strengths directs where you put your time and energy. Doing things in which you're gifted brings delight and passion. By identifying your strengths, you give yourself permission to say "no" to things that aren't your strengths, and "yes" to things that are.

Right now, write down five areas that are your strengths. Is it cooking? Being creative? Organizing? Relationships? Being a listener? Ask

God to help you identify at least five strengths. Don't sell yourself short; don't stop until you have at least five listed.

1.

2.

3.

4.

5.

As we dig deeper, understanding your strengths is foundational in changing expectations, defining priorities, and being free from busyness. It sounds simple because it really is!

But before you concentrate on your strengths, you have to fully surrender your lesser-strengths. The apostle Paul writes about God allowing a weakness in his life so he wouldn't be conceited. God gave Paul the promise of His power being made perfect in his weakness. Therefore, Paul says he will boast even more gladly about his weakness so that Christ's power would rest on him (2 Corinthians 12:9).

Like Paul, God loves us enough to know what's best for us, even when it's uncomfortable.

Most women have a hard time boasting about anything, let alone their weaknesses. Lesser-strengths, when not embraced, make you feel insecure, not confident. Paul's response models a healthy perspective of the weaknesses God allows. By acknowledging God's work where he couldn't succeed on his own, He gave thanks for the weakness because the fullness of Christ's power rested on him.

Do you need Jesus' power to rest on you? Do you want to release your weaknesses to your Creator, confidently trusting that He will fill in the gaps where you're unable?

Let's do that. Take a minute to identify your lesser-strengths. Is it being disorganized? Impatient? Lack of creativity? Speaking before listening? Take a minute and write down a few.

Now, ask God to meet you in those areas. Surrender them to Him. Put them in His hands. Stop loathing your inadequacies.

Being a mom doesn't mean you'll do everything well. Being a balanced mom means living in your strengths and giving yourself grace in your lesser-strengths. It provides you freedom from doing-it-all.

Embracing your God-given strengths is a biblical principle. In 1 Corinthians 12:11, Paul says, "All these are the work of one and the same Spirit, and He distributes them to each one just as He determines" (NIV).

God gives each Christian a function in kingdom work unique to the person, personality, and gifts He's given. He's created your gifts with foresight, thought, and consideration. You were created for a specific purpose, to work alongside your brothers and sisters in Christ. God doesn't want jealousy, insecurity, pride, or false humility to erode your confidence in serving with the strengths He's given you. Will you willingly take your place in God's kingdom as the woman, mother, and royal daughter He's created you to be?

In upcoming chapters, we'll take these foundational principles and build upon them. We'll practically apply them to your priorities, schedule, and life.

Are you ready?

Reflection

Look back at the lesser-strengths you listed earlier in the chapter. Take a moment and surrender them to God. Embrace God's power to work in them. Now, look back at the strengths you wrote down (if you had trouble identifying some, ask a trusted friend or family member to help you).

What surprised you about your strengths?

Which strengths do you feel comfortable in saying, "Yes, this is how God created me. It's okay for me to embrace them!"

How can your strengths begin to define your priorities?

Father, thank you for making me just the way you have - complete in my strengths and lesser-strengths. Holy Spirit, equip me to release the lesser-strengths to Jesus and embrace the gifts you've given me. Use them both for your glory. Amen.

Six

Making It Real

"For when I am weak, then I am strong."
2 Corinthians 12:10b NIV[14]

*N*ow, let's make those strengths and lesser-strengths impact your life.

1. To start, list the family life, parenting, and home-management things you do well.

2. What are your strengths in balancing responsibilities and maintaining order? Write down as many as you can. (Example: Are you good

---

14 New International Version, biblegateway.com

at de-cluttering? Paying bills on time? Do you use technology to organize the family?)

These strengths are now your foundation for prioritizing your time, energy, and busyness. It should guide what you say "yes" and "no" to. For example, if your strength is cooking, but your lesser-strength is organizing, don't offer to organize the PTO carnival. Instead, provide cookies or baked goods. Don't feel guilty about it. There's another mom out there stressing over what to bake for the PTO.

I'm one of them.

3. Now, list things in family life, parenting, and household management that cause anxiety or stress. (Example: Laundry that doesn't end? Disorganization? Kids who don't follow through on chores?) This list is crucial for releasing extra stresses and busyness.

4. Looking at the list, identify things you can minimize, delegate, or let go of. What are chores you despise doing? Who can help you with these? What things can you truly let go?

Take several minutes, even days, to reflect on this. This principle frees you from busyness that robs your gifts from blessing your family and others. Prioritize this list. As we work on other principles throughout the book, come back to this list. Define what you can let go of, and what responsibilities you can share with others.

5. Another question to ask yourself is this: Are there things you're doing because other moms do them? Or because your mom did?

You don't have to do things other women do. If your mom insisted the house was dusted weekly, but you don't care about it, let go of that expectation. Dust once a month instead. Redefine your expectations so they fit you!

6. Now, decide which anxiety-causing items can't be ignored. Prioritize them according to importance. Identify items you can delegate, and those that only you can do.

Remember, your mom-responsibility is to nurture, not to do everything by yourself. Practically speaking, what things on your "anxiety" list can you delegate to your kids, a spouse, or hire out if necessary? As a kid, I remember thinking, "I can't wait to be a mom because then my kids will do my chores." Now that they're old enough to really help out, I'm cashing in that payback!

However, there's an unwritten mom-rule making this step hard. It's the message that mom's supposed to do everything for everyone. But it's an unrealistic expectation. It's unbiblical and causes undue pressure for women. Instead of trying to do everything solo, lessen your anxiety by delegating and minimizing responsibilities.

It's okay to ask for help.

You have more time to nurture and live in your strengths when you give up doing things by yourself.

Now, prioritize the most important things on the "anxiety" list, and let the other things go.

Only You

Releasing and sharing responsibilities means you have more time for things only you can do. In other words:

- Only you can nurture your kids.
- Only you are the wife to your husband.
- Only you can teach your children what you want them to know about life, faith, and family.
- Only you can pick up the pieces of your child's broken heart.
- Only you are responsible for protecting their mind and spirit.

The list can go on. Do you get the picture?

There are moments when you're the only one who can care for the intrinsic needs of your family. These opportunities usually can't be planned ahead of time. When you're too busy with non-essential things, you miss these opportunities with your child.

Other people can teach Bible school or organize the Christmas party.

Only you are a mom to your child, right now.

Applying this principle can be as simple as saying "no" to serving on a committee, or as difficult as changing jobs or setting boundaries with family or friends. When there are conflicts of priorities, ask yourself, "Am I the only one who can fill this need right now? Is it essential for my child or family that I be the one to do this?"

Let that answer guide your decision.

Special Considerations

Some notes about the *only you* principle are important to mention.

The first is what your *true* responsibilities are in meeting the needs of others. The enemy wants you to think it's your job to meet every need of your child or spouse. When you do this, you rob them of opportunities for independence and autonomy. As your children grow, they'll demand less of you for their physical needs, but more of you for their emotional and spiritual needs. An older mom once told me her kids needed her more when they were teenagers than when they were young. I didn't understand what she meant at the time. I couldn't wait for my little ones to get older so they wouldn't be so needy!

As each of my children have approached adolescence, I've realized what she meant. Older kids aren't physically demanding. Instead, they need you to listen, talk, and be emotionally available for them at critical times. When you delegate more responsibilities to your kids and spouse, you're more available when your kids need you mentally, emotionally, or spiritually.

Also, when you try to do it all for others, you rob them of their need for God. Your children and spouse will depend on God *more* when you aren't meeting their every need.

Lastly, if you're meeting people's needs because you don't like saying "no," or letting others down, you're busy for the wrong reasons. Are you pleasing people because you're bound by what they think of you? That's not God's best for you. Overcoming people-pleasing is essential for balanced priorities. It brings freedom and joy. It allows you to overcome insecurities, and be comfortable with who you are. It releases expectations you don't need to put on yourself.

Healthy priorities means you can't do everything for everyone.

Getting It Done

You've identified your strengths, lesser-strengths, anxieties, and needs of others. Let's apply these principles so you can make the lifestyle changes you want.

1. First, what things in your home or routine can you alter to make your life more balanced? Identify the areas you want to work on. What can you do right now to make life more balanced and simple? List five to ten items that would be helpful to change. Keep this list handy. Upcoming chapters will have ideas of how to change your home, routine, and lifestyle to achieve the results you're hoping for.

2. Secondly, what do you need *right now* to have a balanced spirit? Is it self-care? A non-cluttered bedroom, or children who will help out more? Take a few moments to identify the primary needs (physical or emotional) you currently have for balancing life.

3. Third, what truths do you need reminded of as you change priorities? The enemy will lie to you by saying you're selfish if you practice self-care. He'll give you a guilt-trip when you say "no" to something. Counteract that faulty thinking with truth. For example,

   If the lie is: You're a loser because moms should be able do that. *The truth is*: It's okay to say no to that project because it's not my gift.

If the lie is: You're letting them down, again.

The truth is: I don't have to organize the Christmas party because my strength is singing in the choir. That's how I'm serving.

If the lie is: What will people think of you if you don't make an appearance?

The truth is: It's okay if I miss my nephew's ballgame because my daughter is struggling with math. She needs me to help her study for the test tonight.

If the lie is: There's nothing you do well.

The truth is: God's created me this way, and it's good.

What truths can you proclaim to counteract the enemy's lies? List them here:

Closing Thoughts

God is the person whose expectations you need to seek. As you follow the Holy Spirit's wisdom for your priorities, rest in the strengths He's given you. Use them to your advantage. If you're creative, then manage your home with creativity. Bless others with the gifts God's given you. Walk in confidence. Let your "yes" be a joyful "yes," and your "no" be a confident, guilt-free "no."

Finally, don't keep your strengths and new expectations to yourself. If you're married, talk to your husband about these principles. Discuss the things that cause anxiety. Express your needs, asking him to partner with you for a more balanced family life. Delegate responsibilities to your kids. Make household management a family affair. As you set the standard, your kids will adapt. Your kids will enjoy having a happier mom when your stress-load is lighter.

For most of you, these principles will be freeing.

However, if the needs of your husband or kids are complicated because of physical problems or mental health issues, take these principles to God. Ask Him what His expectations are for you. He cares about you and has not forgotten you. Seek discernment for changes in routine, family, or household management from the Holy Spirit. If needed, get input from others. A trusted friend, life coach, or counselor can support you in making healthy changes that honor your gifts, while also meeting the real needs of your family.

If your husband or children's expectations are unrealistic, or if they are physically, emotionally, or verbally abusive, seek professional help. Abusive behavior is not of God. It's never okay.[15]

You're a child of the Most High God and should be respected and honored.

Reflection

Have you answered each of the questions and applications in this chapter? Change happens when you actively participate in planning it. What areas will you work on today?

---

15 1-800-799-7233 is the National Domestic Violence Hotline

How will you release expectations and overcome people-pleasing?

How will you let Jesus fully pour His power into you to accept, implement, and create change in each of these areas? Ask God to release His power in each realm for His glory.

⌒

Dear Jesus, thank you for each of my strengths and lesser-strengths. Empower me to make changes where needed, so my priorities reflect your will for me and my family. Equip me to say "yes" to things you desire, and "no" to things you don't. Give me courage to do the things only I can do for my children, and release things that others can do. Help me to seek your expectations, not others. Amen.

Seven

Parenting in Your Strengths

⌒

"Train up a child…"
Proverbs 22:6

*A*ccepting yourself, prioritizing time, and releasing expectations influences more than household management. It's a holistic approach to life. Balancing life requires you parent in these principles, too.

How do you do this?

You start by establishing a family culture that reflects your gifts and that of your children. Create family activities and traditions that reflect you, your husband, and children. Don't pressure yourself to do what other families do.

If you're creative, family activities might revolve around making crafts. If you're active and like sports, your family might spend more time hiking, biking, or being involved in physical activity. I often remind myself just because one family does something, it doesn't mean I have to create that activity or environment for my family, especially if it's not my strength.

In an age of Instagram, Facebook, and Pinterest, this principle is essential.

When you try to be like other families, you model insecurity and competitiveness. "Keeping up with the Joneses" robs your family of an authentic environment where kids learn acceptance, trust, and family identity. Creating a family culture according to *your* uniqueness builds an environment of freedom, security, and love. Everyone feels safe and can be themselves, including you. Release yourself to build a family culture around *your* strengths, and the strengths of your family.

The Insecurity Trap

Do your insecurities motivate busyness? Are you afraid your kids will be embarrassed by you, or that they compare you to other parents? Though comparison is natural for kids, your worth to them isn't defined by how you measure up with others. They love you because you're *their* mom.

They don't expect you to be Supermom.

Remember? She's not real.

But mom-fears and insecurities are real. When it's my turn to make birthday treats or team meals, I compare myself with other moms. I worry about comments other kids might make. Baking and cooking for school functions causes anxiety, because it's not my strength.

One evening when I was making a cake for a school function, I was multi-tasking. I didn't hear the timer go off. When I pulled the cake out of the oven, it was burned. My self-talk included "loser," and thoughts like "you can't even bake a box-mix without burning it."

After sharing my loser-mom moment on Facebook, a friend suggested I buy a store-bought cake instead of making another one. It challenged the unwritten mom-rule I believed—good moms make things from scratch. It was freeing to hear it was okay to buy a cake and send it to school.

Never has a trip to Walmart been so inspiring.

Since the cake-baking scenario, I've asked my kids to sign me up for simple things like napkins, plates, pop, or chips. They're okay with that. Even when making meals for team sports, my kids reassure me they're okay with what I make.

That's what is most important.

Even if kids complain (because they will), it doesn't define my worth, abilities, or that of my child.

Do you need reminded of that truth?

When I release myself from these fears, it frees up time and guilt. It dispels insecurities. Instead of worrying about a mom-task that's not my strength, I can pour that energy into meaningful time with my child. Instead of the five minutes of fame I'd receive by the "your mom's so cool, look at these cupcakes," my son or daughter would rather have time with me.

Yours would, too.

Defining Priorities

Your strengths should also define other priorities as a parent. What strengths did you identify in chapter five that you can apply to parenting? How can you use them to nurture and engage with your child? List them now:

For example, one of my strengths is spending time with others. When I can't make a sporting event or activity because of work or other responsibilities, I make it a priority to spend time with that child. It might be talking to them at bedtime, or just hanging out with them. Kids don't care as much about what you do with them, as much as they desire a genuine relationship with you.

When you parent in your strengths, you create a family culture with peace and joy from your gifts. Your kids receive more of you. Your relationship with them grows because it's based on being, not doing. You model confidence and security in the process.

Accepting Your Child's Love

Guilt is a great motivator for busyness. Have you ever felt like you've failed your kids, so you spend time and energy trying to make up for things?

Most parents fail their kids at some time or another. When it happens, honesty and authenticity is more important than misplaced priorities or busyness.

Your child still loves you, even when you disappoint them.

Kids see right through false guilt or skewed priorities. If you've messed up or disappointed your child, don't do more to make things right with them. Instead, be honest. When needed, humble yourself and ask for forgiveness. Then, receive their forgiveness and accept their love.

Your kids love you despite your faults, because you're their mom. It doesn't get much better than that.

They want an authentic you; not a perfect or busier you.

Reflection

How can you parent in your strengths and create a unique family culture?

What are you busy with that's motivated by insecurities or guilt instead of authenticity or strengths?

What expectations do you need to let go?

Is there something for which you need to ask your child's forgiveness?

⌣⟩

Father, thank you for the strengths you've given me, and for the opportunity to create a family culture where everyone's gifts can thrive. Thank you for molding our family together with such uniqueness. Show me, also, how to release expectations and create an environment where everyone grows. Help me to be humble and make changes where needed. Amen.

Eight

WHAT'S MOST IMPORTANT

*"Unless the Lord builds the house, those
who build it labor in vain.*

*Unless the Lord watches over the city, the
watchman stays awake in vain."*

PSALM 127:1, ESV[16]

Before we get to the "how to" section of the book, there's one prior-ity that's more important than freezer meals or Pinterest boards. It's knowing your child.

Have you ever considered this an important part of your mom-call-ing? I'm afraid the Supermom image distracts most of us from taking this assignment seriously. We're so busy balancing craziness that we don't see what's most important—our kids. You're not alone in this. I've had more than one student tell me their parents are too busy for them; that their parents don't really know who they are.

I've been guilty of that. Have you?

---

16 English Standard Version, biblegateway.com

What does it mean to know your child? It requires listening to and nurturing them, as we've mentioned in earlier chapters. It's acknowledging their individual strengths, instead of wishing they'd be different. It's protecting them when they're vulnerable. It's meeting their emotional needs at each developmental stage, so they build confidence and strength.

It's a sacred job.

Each of us longs to be known and understood. It's a primary need of human nature. Even though we're sovereignly known by our heavenly Father, that's hard for kids to understand. For proper development, kids need to feel known and understood by their primary caregivers. It makes them feel loved, accepted, secure, and safe. They're able to thrive in relationships and academics. They grow both socially and emotionally.

As a young mom, I heard an impacting message by pastor and Bible teacher Dr. David Jeremiah on his radio program, *Turning Point*. He said he wanted each of his four kids to feel known. He let them know he saw their uniqueness. By acknowledging their individual strengths, he gave his children value.

As the youngest of four kids, I yearned to be seen or heard for who I was, not for my place in the family. This longing contributed to the eating disorder I developed as a young teenager. Over the years, I've struggled to be seen and accepted for who I am. As a parent, I've wanted my kids to know their uniqueness is valued; that they have a special place in our family. Acknowledging your children's strengths and uniqueness is an extraordinary gift you can give them, no matter how many kids you have, or their position in the family.

My mother-in-law, Lois, had a special way of making her kids and grandchildren feel known. She did it through building relationships at her kitchen table, writing notes, and doing special things with them. Though she had thirteen grandchildren over twenty years apart, she understood each one and their special personalities. When she unexpectedly died at sixty-seven, my children were among the youngest grandchildren. I grieved what they missed by not receiving her special love.

In a 4th grade report on heroes, my daughter wrote, "Grandma was kind to the grandkids by always being 'there.' She was always there for me."

Even at young ages, kids know if you're there for them.

My mother-in-law's life and nurturing nature deeply impacted me. After her death, I became more intentional about setting aside time with the kids. Prior to that, I was too busy trying to do it all.

The Simple Things

Time is a precious, cost-free item that lets your kids know you value them. Being present and engaged with them makes time with you special, letting them know you understand and recognize who they are as individuals.

No matter if it's the quantity or quality, a child knows if it's genuine. Simple activities that build intrinsic value with your kids include:

- Reading to your child.
- Praying with them at bedtime, even older kids.
- Asking them about what they're doing, showing interest in their play, schoolwork or other activities.
- Playing games *they* want to play, even when your schedule seems full.
- Taking a child with you while running errands so you have one-on-one time with them.
- Doing a project that's not school-related.
- Coloring with them.
- Talking at bedtime.
- Asking open-ended questions about their day. For example;
  What's one thing you learned at school today?
  What made you laugh today?

Was there anything silly that happened today?
If you could do one thing over today, what would it be?
What made you smile or feel angry today?

- Looking at them in the eyes when they're talking.
- Stooping down to talk or play with them.
- Listening to them, instead of lecturing them.
- Giving them inexpensive items related to their interest.
- Writing a note and putting it on their pillow, in their lunch box, or on the steering wheel of their car.
- Texting your teenagers with encouraging words.
- One-on-one dates with your kids at places or locations that interest them.
- Affirming their strengths before correcting them.
- Asking for forgiveness when you've crushed their spirit.
- Talking positively about them when they're within hearing distance.

The list can be endless.

Just Do It

Nine words have significantly influenced my priorities on time. When I first heard them, I was selling books through a home-party business while being a stay-at-home mom. I was frustrated because ordering, bagging, and delivering the books took a lot of time from my kids for the little profit I received.

I was listening the radio program *Insight for Living* while driving. While teaching on the prophet Daniel, pastor and Bible teacher Chuck Swindoll said,

"Only two things are eternal, God's Word and people."[17]

---

17 Charles Swindoll's lesson on Daniel, from Insight for Living, http://www.insight.org/

That statement confirmed my frustration that the small income I was earning wasn't worth the time it took away from my family. The principle still guides my priorities when temporal things scream louder than the eternal.

What things distract you that don't have eternal value? Your woman-calling as nurturer and life-giver has significant eternal value.

The Power of Being Present

An acquaintance once told me he felt alone as a child, even when his nuclear family was together. He felt disconnected, though his family was around him.

It's a telling picture of many homes where people live together, but don't engage with each other. Meaningful conversations or interactions are absent. It's something to guard against when busyness drives family life.

As a mom, when you're too busy and not present with your kids, they feel it. Often students tell me their mom or dad are "too busy" to talk to them or help them with homework. Even though it may not be accurate, it's how their child perceives them. Sometimes, you need to listen to the cues your child gives you about his or her perception of your priorities.

I had my own wake-up call from my kids when they perceived my priorities were out of balance.

In my mid-thirties, I began running. It was a stress reliever, and the only thirty minutes I had to myself. One day, I looked for my running shoes, but couldn't find them. I looked in all the places I would consciously or absent-mindedly put them. They were nowhere to be found. After looking for a while, I found them hidden in a place where I wouldn't put them.

Someone hid my running shoes.

My husband and children each denied putting them there. To this day, it's a mystery how the shoes got there.

Regardless, one of my kids was telling me, "I don't like when you do that."

The Holy Spirit convicted me. Running had become an idol, a priority that was out of balance. Though it managed my stress, a child sensed running was more important than he or she was.

Do you have idols? You've got more distractions that any prior generation. Smartphones, computers, tablets, social media—they take time and attention away from your children. How much time do you spend interacting with a screen rather than your kids? Ask the Holy Spirit to show you if these or other things take time away from your family.

You can also ask your kids. They'll be real with you. Kids are like that.

Are You Busy?

Normally, kids don't directly tell you when they need you. Instead, they provide subtle messages, like hiding your shoes. Listening for those cues is important. There's one phrase to which you'll want to pay attention. If your child asks, "Are you busy?" it's an open door inviting you into their world. It says, "I need you to see me. Now."

My son recently asked, "Mom, are you busy?" I was in the middle of a project I wanted to finish. "Would you play this with me?" he said.

I looked in the hands of my sixth-grader. He was holding a primitive board game on Andrew Carnegie he made for a school assignment.

"Sure," I said, groaning inside. Playing games is on my most-despised-mom-duty-list.

We sat on the floor, and in ten minutes successfully completed a game about Andrew Carnegie. When we were done, my son had a happy, contented smile. He went downstairs to the man-cave with his brothers, and I returned to the project I was doing earlier.

Those ten minutes were the most important use of my time for the week. Rare are the moments when preteen and teenage boys ask, "Are you busy?"

I remembered days, not too long ago, when I was too busy for a lot of things. I would cringe when the kids asked for my time. I would calculate the cost of putting them off or giving them my attention. I'm thankful when my heart trumps my head. The result is precious time that can't be replaced.

As my son left the room, I longed for more time to spend with each of my kids. Time reading *Mike Mulligan and the Steamshovel*, or rocking them to sleep. I longed for tea parties with my daughter and John Deere tractors to cover my floor.

I'm thankful I gave the right answer to the most important question that night, "Are you busy?"

It's normal to struggle with giving up time when you have little ones under your feet. You wonder if you'll ever have a thought or moment of your own. You wonder if you'll ever have time where someone isn't demanding your energy.

I used to feel that way, too. Now, when one of my kids texts, calls, or asks, "Mom, are you busy?" I recognize the opportunity to be fully present with my not-so-little-ones.

For the harried mom, if I could say one thing you'd take to heart, it would be seeking God's peace and contentment in your season of parenting. While the world seems to be passing you by, it's not. Your children pass by even faster. Once they're self-sufficient, and their world revolves around their peers, you'll long for just a wisp of their presence, and a five-minute conversation to hear their voice.

You'll yearn for time to be fully present.

Ten minutes was all it took to affirm the skill and effort my son put into his project. In a few moments, his capacity for Mom-time was filled.

Later that night, when my other teen boys were in bed, I opened their doors, sat beside them in the dark, and asked if I could pray with them.

They each said, "Sure." So I put my hand on their strong, manly arms, and prayed. They laid still in their beds, with pictures of their girlfriends in the shadows. I kissed their heads, and my heart fluttered when they said, "Goodnight, Mom," as I walked out the door.

Ten minutes was all it took, but my heart was filled. I hope theirs was, too.

Ten minutes is all your kids need for you to be fully theirs, whether they're two, twelve, or twenty.

Living what's important is really that simple. It's ten uninterrupted minutes so you can play a game, help with homework, or know the look in their eyes when they need to talk. It's answering the question, "Are you busy?" with a heart that's fully theirs.

Raising children involves letting them be seen and understood. It equips them to thrive and grow, nurturing them to be successful at each stage of childhood. In today's busy world, you must be intentional to guard your time so it's going where it's needed the most.

You have the task of building and guarding the precious possessions in your home.

Reflection

What's distracting you from seeing and knowing your children? List things that rob your time from your kids.

How can you connect with each of your children, letting them feel unique and special?

What may be out-of-balance idols in your life?

What can you change today to be more engaged with your kids?

⁓

Father, help me see where I'm missing what my children need, emotionally. Equip me to seize the moments that are most important. Teach me to nurture each of my kids in small, yet significant ways. Help me understand what's important in the moment, so I can be intentional with how to spend my time. Amen.

10 Practical Principles for Prioritizing Busyness

Nine

#1 Keeping Marriage Simple

"A new command I give you: Love one another."
John 13:4-35, NIV[18]

In the early years of marriage, my husband and I went to several marriage retreats. We learned about love languages, how our upbringings were different, and ways we could love each other better. We were instructed to have weekly date nights, write post-it-notes on the bathroom mirror, and to prioritize intimacy. We learned about his needs, her needs, how women are like spaghetti, men are like waffles, and how "couch time" is essential once you have kids.

Are you overwhelmed just reading those tips? I was.

As a young bride, an older woman gave me a book instructing me to meet my husband in sexy clothes and go-go boots when he came home from work. Talk about an expectation I didn't feel comfortable with! Within the first few years of marriage, my husband and I read multiple books on how to submit, respect, lead, and pray—more and better. By the end of the first ten years, we were fully equipped for the perfect marriage.

---

18 New International Version, biblegateway.com

Then life happened.

Our family grew, stressors pushed on us, and busyness ruled our lives. We argued more. We accused each other of not meeting each other's needs. Those great how-to's became points of contention over where the other person was failing. As our kids' needs and demands increased, so did our own. Fights revolved around bad communication, busyness, carpool duty, misunderstandings, and physical exhaustion.

Resentment set in. We were often at a stalemate.

In efforts to build a great marriage, we lost perspective of what's most important—how to simply love.

While self-help books on marriage were good, they fed discontentment and unrealistic expectations for a perfect spouse and ideal marriage.

Marriage isn't easy during the parenting years. I wonder if how-to seminars and books create unmet expectations for which spouses blame each other. After twenty-six years of marriage, I've learned balancing marriage and family requires releasing picture-perfect expectations.

Good marriage advice is summed up in four words:

Simply love your husband.

God's Word gives a clear blueprint for loving your spouse. Be kind and patient. Don't be prideful or rude. Don't be easily angered; don't keep records over little things that are petty or unimportant. Rejoice in truth. Protect, hope, and persevere.[19]

Just love your husband. If you need help, pray over 1 Corinthians 13:4-7.

The Exceptions

For most marriages, simply loving will keep things Christ-centered in an already busy and stress-filled life. However, marriage is complicated. There may be emotional baggage one or both of you bring to your relationship. If personal hurts or patterns of relating negatively impact your marriage, don't ignore these issues. Seek healing through professional or pastoral

---

19 1 Corinthians 13:4-7

assistance. Keep the marriage simple by loving your husband while you're working on these issues. Give yourself or your spouse time to heal.

However, if you're in a marriage that is harmful or abusive to you or your children, don't go it alone. Seek help from community agencies trained for abusive situations.[20] God doesn't intend women or children to be disrespected or dishonored.

Abuse is never okay.[21]

God's Plan

Let God work His power in your marriage by letting Him meet your needs instead of your husband.[22] When you expect your spouse to fulfill your needs, you don't allow Jesus to do the intimate work in your life He desires. He wants to draw you close to Him so His Spirit can work in your marriage and family.

God's intention for marriage isn't perfection; it's to represent His character and redemption to the world.

Release expectations that keep your priorities unbalanced. Keep marriage simple, allowing His love to flow through you to your husband.

⌣

Reflection:

What can you do today to simply love your husband?

---

20 The book, The Emotionally Destructive Marriage by Leslie Veronick, can be found at www.leslieveronick.com.

21 The National Domestic Abuse Hotline is 1–800–799–7233.

22 Philippians 4:19

What can you let go that's causing unnecessary stress in your relationship with your husband?

⁓

Dear Father, show me how to simply love my husband. Give me discernment for what to let go of that's causing division in my marriage. Give me wisdom to know when to seek help. Thank you for loving my family. Amen.

Ten

#2 REDEFINING EXPECTATIONS
AND LEARNING TO SAY NO

*There is a time for everything and a season
for every activity under the heavens.*

ECCLESIASTES 3:1 NIV[23]

*K*nowing when to say "yes" and "no" is critical for getting out
of the tightrope lifestyle. Just like saying "no" to your toddler
is important for his or her well-being, saying "no" is important for a
healthy balance of family activities. The culture tells you that you have
to do everything now for your child to be successful. Busyness doesn't
foster success. It creates unbalanced priorities.

It's important to say "yes" and "no" at appropriate times.

The needs of your children change throughout their development.
The current activities you and your children participate in affect your
family's health. It's tempting to get your kids involved in all the available activities for their age. Most kids aren't wired for prolonged busyness and stress. Too many activities can cause anxiety and exhaustion,

---

23 New International Version, biblegateway.com

for kids and adults. As the family manager, you need to say "no" for your child when he or she doesn't understand the level of commitment, busyness, time, and family stress an activity might take.

For a family with more than one child, weighing family needs is important when determining the activities in which individual kids participate. Taking a baby or toddler to practices and games of an older sibling is exhausting for them and you. We made a decision early in our family life to limit each child to two sports or activities per year from elementary through middle school. The kids had to prioritize and choose their activities, considering the needs of their siblings rather than just their own. Even with these guidelines, we often had twenty or more activities in a week between four children.

Does this idea bring fear or apprehension? While society says kids have to do it all to be successful, they don't. Waiting a year or two to start a child in an activity doesn't prevent him or her from excelling in that activity in middle school or high school. Starting a sport at age seven or eight instead of four rarely hurts a child.

Delaying activities can eliminate unnecessary busyness now.

If you're worried that delaying an activity will leave your child behind others, ask God for the best time to get him or her involved. God knows your child's future. He'll guide you in these decisions. He's also able to catch your child up.

Really.

God cares about these things.

When you seek God in all decisions, commitments, and what's best for your family, He will bless and honor your obedience. We've lived this—we've seen God's faithfulness by not compromising His best for the world's fears.

Our kids still have excelled in high school sports and activities, even though we've guarded those opportunities to balance family time, church activities, and health. One child made it to a state championship, and earned the MVP in his second sport. Another child won a full-ride scholarship to any university of his choice in our state. It wasn't because of his athletic ability, but because of volunteer work he did for children with disabilities.

Being on a t-ball team in Kindergarten didn't make a difference for that scholarship board.

As a Christian, trusting God with your child's current and future activities is an act of faith. God isn't removed from these temporal distractions. He's the Author of blessings and outcomes.

Do you need to redefine your expectation for your kids' activities? Are your current activities healthy, or draining on your family? When your kids are young, involve them in a few activities, but leave the real busyness for adolescence.

Teaching your kids to say "no" to unnecessary busyness teaches them security and healthy boundaries. It also allows them, and you, to say "yes" to more important things later.

The activities you're involved in also need examining at various stages. Saying "no" to things which aren't your passion, or gifts, provides more opportunities to say "yes" to things which are. If you're a working mom with kids at home, this may not be the best season to volunteer for committees if it causes extra busyness. If you do, find ones that fit your strengths, and complement your family's schedule. As a full-time working mom, I've given up many church responsibilities because my kids are in after school sports and activities. I've learned there is someone else at a different life stage who can fill a volunteer role.

But no one else can be mom to my kids, or yours. (Remember the "only you" principle?) Take a few minutes to reflect on the following questions:

What can you say "no" to now?

Where can you delegate responsibilities to your children or husband?

How can you take care of yourself by saying "no" to things that overwhelm you?

Home management expectations are also an area to redefine during your current parenting season. When your kids are young, don't expect your house to be picture-perfect. It's messy, and that's okay. It won't be that way forever. When you have teens, there will be sports gear, shoes, homework, and laundry on the floor. This, too, shall pass. So don't stress yourself. Redefine household expectations based on the age of your kids. (We'll cover ways to manage these messes in chapters yet to come.)

Saying "no" also includes not doing things for your kids that they can do for themselves. You're their nurturer, not their maid. Helping your child be self-sufficient and independent at early ages frees up your time and energy to do kingdom work both in and outside of home. When you delegate household tasks to your kids, you have more time for what's important—moments with God, your husband, children, and taking care of yourself.

Just as soon as your kids make messes, they'll be out the door, and your home will be quiet and serene. Even with two of my four children gone, I have more quiet, serene spaces.

You only have your kids for a few years.

You have a lifetime for everything else.

Reflection

Where does your busyness come from? Are your children in activities or sports currently for the wrong reasons?

What fears do you have in saying no to something for yourself or your child?

What things can you eliminate from your family's schedule so you can be more balanced?

Father, equip me to redefine expectations based on my season of parenting. Show me areas in which I need Your wisdom. Thank you for caring about schedules, commitments, and clutter. Help me to see Your perspective. Amen.

Eleven

#3 Don't Parent Alone

"Though one may be overpowered, two can defend themselves. A cord of three strands is not easily broken."

ECCLESIASTES 4:12, NIV[24]

*E*ven though we live an egalitarian era, there's still an unwritten rule that mothers are the primary caretakers of children.

When I was a young mom and would go away for a day or evening without my kids, I was surprised when people asked if my husband was babysitting.

Newsflash—dads don't babysit! Babysitters are people you pay to watch your kids, who aren't Mom or Dad.

Regardless of your beliefs about men and women's roles, there's a universal truth about God's family plan: Parenting is a partnership, just like marriage. Both you and your child's father are responsible to raise them. This includes spending time with that child, teaching them, and taking care of their physical, spiritual, and emotional needs. While your

---

24 New International Version, biblegateway.com

primary mom-role is nurturing your child, both you and your child's father work together to parent and take care of their needs.

If you're married, this involves communicating your needs and parenting expectations with your husband. It doesn't matter whether you're working away from the home or in the home, you both have active roles in care-taking. Talk with your husband about principles in this book. Share your strengths, lesser-strengths, stresses, and anxieties with him. Suggest areas where he can help so you and your family can achieve better balance.

Do you need help with meal preparation? Clean up? Getting kids to and from practices? What about expectations? Are there expectations you're putting on yourself that you think your husband expects of you? Talk with him about it. You might find he doesn't really care about the things you think he does. Talk honestly with him, then work together as a team.

If problems in your marriage make this conversation difficult, talk with a trusted friend or mentor about how to begin the conversation. Seek God. Ask for His timing, words, and wisdom. Don't dismiss this step without giving it a try (except for abusive situations, in which professional help should be sought). Don't shy away from conflict. Decide what areas are essential to talk to your child's father about, and see what doors may open. Even if your child's father isn't receptive, you're identifying and speaking about your needs, self-care, and anxieties.

You're learning how to take care of yourself.

When I was most stressed, I was doing the housework, finances, cooking, laundry, grocery shopping, and carpool errands by myself, while working full time. When I honestly shared my struggles with my husband, he responded with, "How can I help?" We spoke about expectations we had of each other, which lowered my stress. Most of the expectations I had were ones I put on myself.

We agreed on two areas of which he would take over primary responsibility. We started working together, and I wasn't doing it all anymore.

Taking the risk to share my needs created a parenting partnership. Though your conversation may have different results, it's a step towards better balance, expressing your needs, and modeling how parents work together.

If you're a single mom, God doesn't intend for you to parent alone, either. If your child's father is approachable, consider having a similar conversation. If his or her father is absent, allow others to partner with you on the parenting journey. Don't parent alone.

Whatever circumstances have brought you to single parenting, God has created community around you to support you and your child.[25] Don't be afraid to reach out to family, friends, church, or the broader community who care for you and your children. Don't isolate yourself. Reach out by grabbing hold of your strengths, and the strengths of the others. Let go of non-essential stresses.

Single or married, where can you reach out so you're not parenting alone? What can you delegate or give up? How can *you* have a conversation for change?

Reflection

What do you need to share with your husband or child's father about stresses, anxieties, or how he can help you in parenting tasks? When will you talk to him? Write down a time so you can hold yourself accountable.

---

25 A great resource is Jennifer DeMaggio's *Life Of A Single Mom* ministry

If you're a single mom, what are your biggest needs? Who can you reach out to?

Father, equip me to have a conversation with others about my needs, and how others can help so I'm not parenting alone. Thank you for giving me permission to take care of myself, to look to You to provide creative ways to take care of my needs. Amen.

Twelve

#4 Managing Your Home So It Works for You

"She provides food for her family and portions for her servant girls."
Proverbs 31:15, NIV[26]

e've covered a lot of material so far. Some of it may seem overwhelming or out of reach. It's not. Each principle can balance and change your priorities. Apply them, one by one, to your life.

The next few chapters provide practical how-to's you can start now. While we'll suggest tips to make your home more manageable, the most important principle comes down to one thing:

Find what works for you.

To start, here are four practical ideas for managing your house so it works *for you*, not against you:

1. *Make your space work for your family during your current phase of life.* Don't let the size of your space deter you from being organized or controlling clutter. Be creative, even with small spaces, so that messiness isn't overwhelming. If you have small kids and need

---

26 New International Version, biblegateway.com

storage for toys, find attractive boxes, baskets, or bins to store toys that blend with your living space. With storage containers accessible, you can easily pick up toys or clutter and be ready for guests in a matter of minutes. Store breakable items out of reach so you don't have to worry about kids getting into things you don't want broken. Make your space friendly for the age of kids you have in your home, changing your storage needs as they grow.

2. *Think differently about your space.* What are your current needs for organization or home management? Considering your needs, determine how you can use space more efficiently, how you can redesign spaces so they're more efficient for you and your family.

   For a while, our computer and homework space was in the kitchen and dining area, so I could help kids with homework while making dinner. At another time, that space was in our laundry room, so I could work on lesson plans and answer emails while doing laundry. Where do you need your home office or homework center to be? Look at unused space in your home. How you can utilize it other than how it's currently being used?

   Another tip is re-arranging kitchen storage at different ages so kids can easily reach plates, bowls, and silverware. Make storage containers accessible so they can put away dishes. My Tupperware lid drawer is never organized, but the kids have unloaded the dishwasher since they were in kindergarten. That trade-off is important to me!

3. *Delegate tasks.* In addition to sharing responsibilities with your husband, also involve your kids. Once your kids are preschool-age, they can perform a variety of tasks; emptying wastebaskets, drying dishes, picking up, and putting their clothes away. What chores and responsibilities can you give your children so they're helping the family unit? Expect them to follow through.

4. *Weigh the cost of doing everything yourself.* There's nothing godly about doing work all by yourself. Many women have told me how freeing this statement is for them. Generation after generation,

women are taught to believe you have to do it all, that you're somehow lazy or less than enough if you ask for help.

Being a helpmate to your husband doesn't mean he, or others, are exempt from helping you.

In addition to delegating tasks to your husband and children, there may be times to hire outside services, if it's affordable. It's a trade-off that helps with managing responsibilities in and outside of home. You're the household manager—you don't have to do all the work yourself. That's the example of the Proverbs 31 woman. She *managed* her home well. She didn't do all of it herself.

Put guilt aside and don't worry about what others think.

Remember, God wants us to be nurturers in His kingdom. Managing your home doesn't mean striving for more things to do. Managing well means you're creating an environment of peace, serenity, and love.

The home belongs to everyone, and everyone maintains the home. Find what works best for you. Whether you delegate chores, rearrange space, hire outside help, or let go of expectations, find what fits your family and reduces your stress levels so you can live best in the busyness.

Reflection

What household tasks can you delegate to make life more manageable? To whom will you delegate them?

What areas of the home need better organization or modification to fit your season of life?

What three things can you work on in the immediate future to make your house more manageable?

    1.

    2.

    3.

Father, thank you for not expecting me to do all these things alone. Help me to first and foremost make my home a place of nurture, serenity, and peace. Equip me to manage it well, changing things as needed, delegating where I can, and being creative to make it a place of comfort, not dread. Thank you for making my house a home. Amen.

Thirteen

#5 Keeping Order Without Losing Your Mind

*"And may the peace of God that passes all understanding
guard your heart and mind in Christ Jesus."*
PHILIPPIANS 4:6, NIV[27]

"You'll know how I'm doing by what my apartment looks like," Ashley said. Her life reflected her apartment's chaos. She was a single mom I was serving as a home-based therapist for families in foster care. Sorting clothes or washing dishes were some of the most therapeutic things we did together as we made sense of her mental, behavioral, and emotional needs. As her physical surroundings became less chaotic, she was better able to cope with life and parenting.

As moms, you and I have similar needs. Order in physical surroundings makes it easier to handle demands of parenting, work, stress, and life. When too many responsibilities hit you at once, you're overwhelmed. You don't know where to start tackling things. Bills, ballgames, work—everything creates stress. When overwhelmed, it's easy to take your stress out on your kids.

---

27 New International Version, biblegateway.com

Have you ever done that? I have. How do you keep order without losing your mind?

Understanding yourself and knowing your limits is one place to start.

When you identify what you need for peace of mind in your home, it's easier to prioritize these and let other things go. What things can you minimize around your home that cause you stress? How can you organize things to save time and energy, while managing your family?

In understanding needs and limits, here are suggestions that help moms balance emotional, mental, and physical responsibilities:

1. *Identify where order is essential.* For me, order in certain areas reduces my stress; the bedroom, laundry room, kitchen counter, and the kitchen table are my essential places. When these areas are clutter-free, I feel like the house is intact, even if other places are messy. Baskets for paper and homework are helpful. Picking up the family room at the end of a day also helps start the next day with peace of mind.

   Where are the essential areas for order in your home?

2. *Simplify important tasks.* Clean surfaces and floors are two of my non-negotiables for keeping the house clean. Keeping anti-bacterial wipes in the bathrooms, kitchen, and the laundry room make for easy clean-up. With three teenage boys at home, our toilets are cleaned daily, but it only takes a few minutes. You can also take a few minutes to sweep a dirty floor in between regular cleanings. These simple tasks make a difference in our busy lives, where dirt

compounds, and time to deep clean is limited. What important tasks can you simplify?

3. *De-clutter a few minutes each day.* When the kids were young, we had large, decorative baskets, or crates, in various rooms for toys. Twice a day, during nap-time and before bed, I'd put toys in baskets or bins so I wasn't overwhelmed the next morning. Now, this happens with shoes, gym bags, books, and miscellaneous items. Picking up only takes a few minutes. You can find cheap storage containers at garage sales, thrift, or discount stores. Having them available makes de-cluttering easy!

Where can you store things for quick clean up? What items do you need to make this happen?

4. *Eliminate perfection.* Each room in our home isn't neat, organized, or picked up. The kids' rooms are usually a mess, but I can shut their doors so I don't see it. I don't mind how they put their clothes away, as long as they do it. Kitchen drawers are unorganized, but the kids put the dishes away. That's a trade-off I value. These are a few of my "non-essentials" for less-than-perfect housekeeping. What are yours?

5. *Choose your battles.* Choosing your battles isn't a concept confined to discipline. It's also important for prioritizing busyness, self-care

and balance. Instead of doing it all, where should you spend your limited time?

Like the other principles, battles with your children over household chores should be relative to their age. When my children were small, I gave up the struggle of having bedrooms picked up, knowing when kids got older, those expectations would be more realistic. Doing laundry, however, is an expectation I follow through on. Starting at age five, our kids put their clothes away to the best of their ability. Clothes don't have to be hung up perfectly, or in their drawers nice and neat; but it needs to be done. For me, it's a chore that's important for them to complete.

These are just two examples of battles I've chosen, and expectations I've released. What are expectations you can let go of to reduce stress or busyness? What stress can you eliminate for this season of parenting, giving you more time for rest, self-care, or relationships?

6. *Make hard decisions.* As you consider your battles, you may find yourself facing lifestyle decisions. When I was teaching 180 high school students, and parenting four children from elementary to high school, it took a toll on my mental and emotional health. Stress levels, busyness, and lack of self-care left me emotionally exhausted. I was reactionary, irritated, and frustrated with my family on a consistent basis.

I wasn't the mom I wanted to be.

While appearances looked good, I was falling apart inside. Instead of continuing to battle the busyness, stress, and exhaustion, I needed a job with different options to better fit our stage of life.

I made a hard decision to give up teaching. I went back to graduate school, full time, to obtain a degree with better work options for our family. That decision made a radical difference in our family because it changed me. I now have time to rest and breathe. I have mental space that makes me a calmer woman, wife, and mom.

Choosing your battle is important. It may be risky. But if it creates better balance, it's worth it.

Your kids sense your stress levels. What battles might you need to fight, alter, or give up in order to have peace of mind, heart, and home?

Reflection

Before you answer the following questions, ask the Holy Spirit to speak to you, giving you wisdom and clarity.

What are your top priorities for this season of parenting? List three of them.

1.

2.

3.

What tasks are important in keeping your stress levels down? What are the essential areas of your home where you need order?

Where is perfectionism getting in the way of basic household needs?

What expectations you can let go of to reduce stress or busyness?

What stress can you eliminate for this season of parenting, giving you more time for rest, self-care, or relationships?

Dear Lord, thank you for your love. Thank you for giving clarity to my life, helping me prioritize things that need to be modified or changed during this season of life. Empower me to make needed changes. Amen.

Fourteen

#6 The Never Ending To-Do-List

Lord, don't you care I'm left to do all this work by myself?

LUKE 10:40, PARAPHRASE

Have you ever walked around the house for several minutes, or hours, without completing a task? I have. Some days, making lunch, picking up toys, changing diapers, and carpooling kids is all you accomplish. Do you wonder how to get anything but the immediate demands accomplished?

Do you have a never-ending list of things to get done?

A young mom once showed me her "to do" list. "Where do I start?" she asked.

Lists are helpful for focusing on what has to be done both at work and home. They're also overwhelming if you make them more important than their function. You don't need more stress to complete the list.

No matter if you use paper and pencil, an app, or another organizing tool, the important thing is finding something that works for you.

Here are tips for managing lists while being a busy mom.

1. *Compartmentalize.* Most women multitask. However, this can be counter-productive if you don't manage it. Because of the various roles and responsibilities you have, multitasking can be a downfall if you don't focus on what's needed in the moment. It's helpful to separate various responsibilities. For example, I have an *at work* list, an *at home* list, and a *ministry* list. When you focus on domains individually, it prevents getting distracted by other responsibilities.

2. *Prioritize.* I have informal categories for the lists mentioned above, whether they're on paper, a phone, or on an electronic post-it. One category is for items to be done within a day or two. This includes bills to pay, people to contact, appointments to make, etc.

   Another category is a to-be-done-soon list. This list helps to plan ahead and combine errands throughout the week. By the end of the week, you mark completed items, and start a new list.

   A third category includes goals to accomplish in the near future. If you're like me, if I don't write my goals down, they don't happen. Dreams stay in your mind, but goals are things you put words and actions to. This list makes "want-to's" a reality. Goals on this list might include painting a room, meeting a far-away friend, teaching a Bible study, or writing a book.

3. *Simplify.* Keep your lists short, simple, and to the point.

4. *Delegate.* Remember, your job is managing your family and home, not doing everything yourself. Lists help your kids manage time, responsibilities, and chores, too. Younger kids feel empowered, confident, and responsible when you give them a list with things to accomplish. I love seeing a child's pride in completing a job *their* way. It fosters independence.

   Lists also decrease fights between siblings who otherwise tell each other who should do what. When making a list, I often specify who is responsible for each chore.

Another bonus of lists is sending teenagers on errands once they can drive. It's a great learning experience, usually resulting in humorous stories.

5. *Personalize.* These strategies work for me, but they may not work for you. Find what works for you, and do it! More important than list-making, is prioritizing essential things to balance your life. Laundry, cooking, and errands won't go away. Finding the best way to manage responsibilities is most important.

6. *Give yourself grace.* Some people avoid lists because of anxiety. A list is an organizing tool to prioritize and stay focused, not to condemn or cause more stress.

The bottom line: find what works for you and your family, and do it.

Reflection
What organizing tool works best for you?

How can you use that tool to better manage your tasks and busyness?

What would you like to accomplish that you're afraid to write down? Consider starting a "goal" list for the things you put off because busyness distracts you.

Father, thank you for caring about simple things like lists, organizing my home, and helping me to get simple things done. Help me find what works for me so I have more time with you, my family, and taking care of myself. Thank you.

Fifteen

#7 Tips for Tackling the Outdoors

⁓

…"See how the flowers of the field grow. They do not labor or spin. Yet I tell you that not even Solomon in all his splendor was dressed like one of these."

Matthew 6:28a -29, NIV[28]

If you have a yard, a few flowers, or a garden, these also take time, energy, and effort to maintain. How do you manage outdoor responsibilities, in addition to everything else?

The same way you do other things—with determination, creativity, and teamwork.

Mowing the lawn and raking leaves with babies and toddlers requires innovative ideas. Port-a-cribs, baby swings, baby slings, and backpacks are useful. Toddlers and preschoolers can push toy mowers, or ride toddler toys with wheels. Older kids can plant seeds, pull weeds, and water flowers. Eventually, they'll be mowing the lawn!

While tablets or phones keep kids busy, children need physical play for their social, emotional, and intellectual development. Kids are

---

28 New International Version, biblegateway.com

created to run and tumble. While you're working outside, let them play, get dirty, and safely explore within your yard. Physical activity is good for them. Give them a bowl, a spoon, and a cup, and let their imagination go wild! Sidewalk chalk, bubbles, play-dishes, or a sandbox keep kids occupied and fosters creativity. A favorite activity from my childhood is draping a blanket over a clothesline to make a tent. Let your kids explore and play outside—it's a gift!

For you, working outdoors can be a time for prayer, mental rest, and connecting with nature. Use the time to rest your spirit.

Don't be afraid to embrace the possibilities of working outside with your kids. Use the time to engage with them, developing a love for the outdoors, and creative play. You're sowing seeds in their intellectual, emotional, and physical development by giving them activities with nature.

How can you overcome your challenges of working outside?

Reflection

What simple, outdoor activities can your kids do with you?

What holds you back from allowing your kids to explore the outdoors?

What outdoor chores can your children begin doing now?

～

Father, thank you for outdoor beauty that reflects Your glory and majesty. Help me approach outside work as an opportunity to spend time with You, to rest my heart, while letting my kids be active. Give me a new, joyful perspective on working outside. Thank You for caring for these smallest details. Amen.

Sixteen

#8 Helpful Hints from Seasoned Moms

"Then they can train the younger women..."
Titus 2:4, NIV[29]

I didn't know much as a young bride. Scrambled eggs and macaroni and cheese was all I knew how to cook. The first time I hung clothes on the clothesline, I realized I didn't have any clothespins. They were always in a bag on my mom's clothesline. I didn't know how to plant flowers, preserve vegetables, or take care of a baby.

I'm thankful for learning things from experienced moms. I've seen women with small homes provide generous hospitality—showing that an open door, and heart, is really what matters. I've been mentored at kitchen tables by women with a Titus 2 spirit.

"Guide older women into lives of reverence so they end up as neither gossips nor drunks, but models of goodness. By looking at them, the younger women will know how to love their husbands and children, be virtuous and pure, keep a good house, be good wives." Titus 2:3-4, The Message[30]

---

29 New International Version, biblegateway.com
30 The Message, biblegateway.com

Observing godly mentors has impacted every part of my life. One thing I've learned from older women is that managing a house doesn't have to be a burden. Through simple tasks, housekeeping can be easy, giving more time for relationships, sharing Jesus, and a full life.

What better way to be equipped than to learn household tips from mentors, seasoned moms, and personal experiences. I asked several women the question, "What's helped you in managing house and home?" Here are their answers. While these principles aren't "one-size-fits-all," find the ones that help you!

Meal plan and freezer cook. Many women, myself included, cook several meals at one time and freeze them. In three to four hours you can produce anywhere from six to twenty meals. By using basic ingredients like ground beef, chicken, rice, or vegetables, you can make several meals in a short amount of time. For meal planning, one busy mom recommends emeals.com. I often try simple variations of recipes, substituting different vegetables, potatoes, or meat. Freezer cooking can be as elaborate or as simple as you need it to be.

Bulk cook. Cooking batches of hamburger, rice, soup, or other staples at one time, and freezing them, also decreases preparation time when you need a home-cooked meal.

Preserve food. You don't need a big garden to preserve food. Canning or freezing small batches of in-season fruits or vegetables from a farmer's market works if you don't grow it yourself.

Use a crock-pot. It's great for cooking meals while you're at work or running errands.

Teach your kids to do their own laundry. Several moms have kids do their own laundry—even as young as age eight. It's one task that's completely do-able.

Teach your kids to help with household chores. There isn't a perfect formula for kids doing chores, but if you set the expectations, your kids will rise to the task. Our philosophy of chores is family-centered—we all help because we're part of the family unit.

Teach your kids to pick up after themselves. Once kids are old enough to clean up after themselves, let them do it. From picking up toys, to cleaning a bathroom, you're teaching them responsibility and independence.

Rest. Though it sounds contradictory, resting decreases busyness. Rest helps your physical, mental, and emotional health. It reduces stress. Instead of pushing yourself and not getting enough sleep, get adequate rest. Nap if needed, so you have energy to get necessary things done.

Plan your busyness. As much as you can, plan errands and appointments on the same day, coordinating them with other events (sporting events, lessons, etc.). This gives you more time at home and less time in the car.

Plan time for productive multitasking. Use waiting time at a ballgame, doctor's office, or in the pick-up line to fill out paperwork, make appointments, answer emails, or other simple tasks. These are my favorite places to fill out various school forms kids get during the year.

Use the ten minute rule. Spend a few minutes, each day, doing minor tasks that otherwise build up—putting dishes or clothes away, straightening up a desk, a toy corner, etc. Rotate rooms where you spend 10-15 minutes a day decluttering a particular area. It's amazing how ten productive minutes brings peace of mind. Take ten minutes decluttering instead of checking social media. Look for idle pockets of time you can use to your advantage.

Make a game out of dreaded chores. Play "match the sock game" for mismatched socks that build up over time. Dump the mismatched-socks in the middle of the floor and give small rewards for the amount of socks the kids match. Also, have kids join you for big chores you don't like to do—even at young ages these chores can be fun. Give them a treat when you're done. You'd be surprised how much kids enjoy helping Mom.

Keep cleaning supplies stocked in high traffic areas—like bathrooms, the kitchen, toy rooms, the nursery, or the laundry room. Disinfecting wipes quickly clean a toilet, sink, dirty smudges, fingerprints, food, and other childhood messes in a short amount of time. Cleaning sink and toilet surfaces daily only takes about a minute.

Routinely sweep high traffic areas. The ten-minute rule applies to sweeping, too. Take ten minutes to sweep high traffic areas between regular cleanings. It makes your house cleaner for kids, and provides peace of mind.

Let things go. Managing a house doesn't mean having things spotless. It's prioritizing the most essential things for your household and family, now. It's giving yourself grace to let other things go. Household priorities will differ from woman to woman. Eliminate things which don't need to be done today, tomorrow, or even in this season of life. Then, give yourself grace.

Reflection
Choose three to five tips mentioned that may help you.

1.

2.

3.

4.

5.

What is needed to implement them?

1.

2.

3.

4.

5.

Dear Father, equip me to use time wisely so I have more time to rest and be refreshed. Show me practical ways I can manage our time and responsibilities so we have more time for what's important. Amen.

Seventeen

#9 SIMPLE INVESTMENTS IN FAMILY ACTIVITIES

*"Do not store up for yourselves treasures on earth,
where moths and vermin destroy, and where thieves
break in and steal. But store up for yourselves treasures
in heaven, where moths and vermin do not destroy,
and where thieves do not break in and steal. For where
your treasure is, there your heart will be also."*

MATTHEW 6:19-21, NIV[31]

First comes love, then comes marriage, then comes baby in the carriage. Then what?

Then you work hard to pay for things your kids need. You get them the best education, the latest technology, and position them to fit in with the right crowd. You save for college, and make sure they get into the right university. You want them to have what you didn't have, to make the team. To live happily ever after.

If you're heavily investing in these things, you'll be disappointed. While these goals are good, if you spend the parenting years striving

---

31 New International Version, biblegateway.com

for outward success, you'll miss the biggest investment of all—developing faith, relationships, and memories with your kids.

While your family is young and your children are home, make time for what's intrinsically and eternally important. Family moments don't have to be long, expensive, or elaborate. Finding a few minutes to do a memorable activity brings balance and perspective in a busy schedule.

Special times your children have with you and their siblings builds security and connection. It makes family and home a safe, accepted place to be. Here are investments that have intrinsic value:

A dress-up box. A box full of play clothes and costumes can provide hours of fun for kids and their friends. Kids can play house, use them for Halloween parties, and put on homemade productions. Fill a box with old clothes, Halloween costumes, or items from Goodwill, and let your children be creative!

A scavenger hunt. Take your kids on a scavenger hunt either around your house or yard. Kids love searching for clues, finding things in nature, or things you've hidden. Create a theme. Have older siblings design a scavenger hunt for younger kids.

Picnics. Eating outside on a blanket makes an everyday meal something special. You don't have to go to a park or different location—picnics in your yard are memorable, too. Put a special trinket or sticker in the bottom of the lunch bag as a secret prize. Or allow kids to pack their own bag or lunch box. Sit on a blanket or in a tent in your yard. Talk about the sights and sounds around you. Pretend you're on a ship or magic carpet. Engage your imagination with your kids. During winter months or on a rainy day, have a picnic inside by doing the same things, only on the living room floor instead.

Books. Books provide special moments at nap or bedtime. They contribute to academic success and personal connection. When our kids were in elementary school, I chose several books and Christian biographies I hoped they would read to shape their worldview and Christian development. Each book had a dollar value. When they finished reading a book, they wrote something they learned from the book on coupons we made. The kids cashed the coupons in for things they wanted to purchase—like other books, appropriate video games, trinkets, or other special items. Do the same things with library books, or other books you'd like your kids to read. My kids have mentioned how biographies of church leaders and missionaries from this project have impacted their faith.

Audio stories. While tablets and YouTube videos provide hours of entertainment, audio books provide higher-level thinking and foster a child's imagination. They provide stories you can enjoy together as a family while traveling. Our favorite audio stories are the *Adventure In Odyssey* series from Focus on the Family. Over the years, this resource has been the kids' the most requested gift for birthdays and holidays. They've learned things about God, life, history, and the Bible from the stories and characters. Even our teenagers still listen to them. Each of the kids have said what an impact the stories and the lessons have had on them. We even were able to take a family vacation to the Focus on the Family headquarters in Colorado Springs, Colorado, to visit Whit's End. It was a special experience for our family.

Dates with kids. Taking your kids on dates by yourself or with your husband deepens your relationship with them. You get a window into your child's world, no matter their age. During the summer, I try to take each child on an individual date. These outings have been filled with laughter, silliness, flat bike tires, and lost cars in a rainstorm. Several of the ideas in the next section can also be used for dates with your kids.

Family outings or vacations. Vacations are essential to get away from work. They can be low-cost. Each summer, we've gone somewhere, even if it's a short distance away. While family trips include whining and fighting, they also provide memories, laughter, and family bonding.

Family outings don't have to be expensive. Here are ideas that span a range of ages and interests:

Visiting children's museums that have spaces for babies and toddlers, in addition to activities for older children.

Safe outdoor activities for the whole family. Hiking, riding bikes, visiting parks, or finding summer programs for kids allows the wonder of nature to entertain them. These activities may require special baby gear, but it allows you to interact with all of your kids *and* nature.

Camping outdoors at your house is a fun and practical way to go away overnight. You have the conveniences of home (bathrooms, water, and beds if children don't sleep well), but you don't have the hassle of packing items for young kids. It's a camping experience that's user-friendly for everyone.

Visiting amusement or water parks with rides for both young and older children creates a day the whole family enjoys.

Playing outdoor games in your yard is inexpensive fun. Croquet sets, playing corn hole, or making your own obstacle course are activities all kids can be a part of.

Planning a trip to a beach entertains all kids. Even if the water is cold, you can build sand structures and play beach games.

Holding outdoor movie nights is fun. Spread a blanket on the ground, make popcorn, and use your laptop or tablet to watch a movie.

Having a graffiti day. Using washable markers made for glass, let your kids write, draw, or color on your windows. Have a cookout and let the kids decorate the windows together. Kids can clean up the following day, and learn responsibility in the process.

Having an outdoor dance party is memorable for kids. Plug speakers into your iPod or phone, get some party leis, tropical-themed paper plates, and turn a cookout into a family dance-a-thon, complete with a mamba line or limbo game.

Having a "staycation" where you don't go away, but do special things at home for a day or weekend. Stay in your pajamas, play board games, or have a movie marathon. Make crafts or have a gaming tournament. Whatever you do, put other responsibilities aside, and have an in-house vacation with your kids.

Visiting local businesses or attractions you've never visited before. We've found hidden treasures in our community by visiting local restaurants, stores, parks, and other businesses we normally don't visit. These excursions are close to home—an asset for smaller kids who become tired or cranky.

⸻

Reflection
What can you do to be present with your kids?

What holds you back from having fun with them?

Choose two or three activities you can do with your family in the immediate future. What would you like to do?

1.

2.

3.

⸻

Father, equip me to make time for small investments with my kids, even when I don't think it's possible. Help me find simple things to build memories and laughter with them. Amen.

Eighteen

#10 Special Words for Working Moms

"A woman who fears the Lord is to be praised."
PROVERBS 31:30B, NIV[32]

Whether you're working full-time with a home-based business, part-time, or full-time outside of home, it's hard to find the perfect balance as a working mom. That's because there's no magic formula. The most important thing is that you find what works for you and your family. You don't need extra guilt because you don't do things the way others do them.

Here are words of experience to working mom with kids still at home:

1. *Don't expect to do everything you did before you were working or working without kids.* It's not possible. Give yourself grace as you figure out your season of being a working mom.
2. *Talk with your husband about your needs.* You can't do it all and shouldn't be expected to. Make household and family

---

32 New International Version, biblegateway.com

management a partnership, just like other areas of marriage. Divide responsibilities. It's okay to say, "I can't do it all" and expect a team approach to household management. Remember, marriage is a partnership.

3. *Realize that working in or outside the home doesn't define you as a Christian woman.* When I first worked outside the home, I asked God, "Show me how to be the Christian woman you desire me to be." His answer was that a woman's identity is not dependent upon working in or outside the home. Your identity is in being His daughter. (Revisit the first chapters on Christ-centered identity).

4. *Have more fun with your kids.* Your job and household responsibilities quickly consumes time and energy. Do simple, fun things with your kids. Go out to breakfast before school. Stop for ice cream for no reason, other than it's out of your routine. You may not have warm cookies when they come home from school, but you're creating warm, happy memories with them.

5. *Have an organizational system that meets your family's needs.* When you have multiple kids, organization is essential. For example, each of our kids have their own drawer in a plastic bin for shoes, sports equipment, and other things belonging to them. Whether it's homework, papers to return to school, or keys once they're driving, find simple organizational tools that work for your space and needs.

6. *Have a cooking day and put meals in the freezer.* For me, this is a great investment of time.

7. *Do laundry during the week.* Saturdays are filled with kids activities, sporting events, and household chores. Instead of being overwhelmed by laundry, too, wash clothes during the week so there's more downtime on weekends.

8. *Seek God's approval, not others'.* You'll face judgment from someone for working, or for being too busy while you've got kids at home. When this happens, let those opinions go. Focus on

your relationship with Christ, and what He says about you. The decision to work in or outside the home is between you and your husband, or you and your children if you're a single parent. Other people don't need to know your reasons or your financial situations. You're accountable to God and your family, first. Rest in that.

9. *Above all else, find what works for you.* All of these suggestions may or may not work for you. The important thing is creating a healthy balance between work and home—including time for yourself.

Reflection

What are the things you struggle with most as a working mom? List them.

Prayerfully, give them to Jesus. Ask Him to equip you to handle these stresses.

Which suggestions will you implement?

Dear Lord, help me find things that work best for me as I work either in or out of home. Equip me to take care of practical needs that help me have time with my family and personal rest. Thank you for taking care of me. Amen.

The Important Things

Nineteen

DON'T STEAL THE STRUGGLE

⌐

"...We know that suffering produces perseverance;
perseverance, character; and character, hope."[33]
ROMANS 5:3B-4, NIV

*H*ave you ever thought once your child reaches adulthood, you're done parenting? I have. For eighteen years or more you give your time and energy for immediate needs—making costumes, buying sports gear, signing report cards, and screening dates. Busyness takes care of the here and now, easily distracting you from the bigger picture of parenting.

Parenting isn't about the cap and gown. It isn't muddling through until they reach graduation. It's equipping them with values, character, and perseverance for a lifetime. Yet diapers, trips to Walmart, and immediate demands sidetrack long-term parenting goals. Do you find yourself giving up in the moment, so you can get on with what's next?

Worse yet: Do you give into your child's momentary discomfort just so they're happy? Do you avoid dealing with situations?

---

33 New International Version, biblegateway.com

It's easier to do things for kids instead of allowing them to struggle. Whether it's tying their shoes, learning multiplication, ending a friendship, or facing consequences of a poor decision, it's tempting to rescue kids from difficulties. When you do this, you rescue them from valuable lessons, and make more work for yourself.

Don't Steal the Struggle

Regardless of their age, or circumstances, seeing your kids suffer is never easy. Romans 5:3-5 says that suffering produces perseverance, perseverance produces character, and character produces hope. It's an encouraging and powerful verse because it gives hope to the fears you have about suffering. Not only does your child benefit from persevering through suffering, they gain character and hope from overcoming trials.

When your child has adversity, don't steal their struggle.

When they figure out a difficult task, kids problem-solve, develop endurance, and overcome temporary pain. They learn confidence, new skills, perseverance, and responsibility. In turn, you gain assurance, knowing they can figure things out and be independent.

However, when you steal their struggle, they lack what it takes to overcome adversity. They don't learn the power of victory, and the hard work it takes to get there. Your natural instinct is to protect your kids in all circumstances. When you do this, you rob them of skills needed when you're not around. You short-change their growth potential, no matter their age.

Developing a tenacity to overcome struggle equips your child for pain that life brings them.

What benefits have you gained from overcoming hardships? I've received determination and strength. Our kids have grown from adversity in sports, relationships, jobs, and academia. They've learned fairness can be arbitrary. Those are hard lessons, even for adults!

It's better for kids to know pain and adversity when they're still at home, where you can guide and support them. Learning about unfairness, perseverance, and problem-solving as an adult can be a rude awakening to life's realities.

Don't steal the struggles your kids need to be strong, healthy adults.

The Dangers of Enabling

Enabling is a growing problem affecting families. It creeps into homes, even Christian ones. In efforts to make your kids happy and successful, you remove what's uncomfortable and painful. You steal their struggle, avoiding negative outcomes at all costs.

You rob your child of their need for God.

God doesn't remove pain from our earthly experience. "Health and wealth" Christianity confuses well-meaning parents about truth, God's character, and His Word. While God pours blessing and goodness on His children, He doesn't shield us from struggle. Instead, He meets us in the pain.

Enabling happens when a person facilitates or supports someone else's behavior. Though well-meaning, it keeps children and adults trapped in unhealthy, immature, or irresponsible behavior. It prevents them from growing, persevering, and changing. Enabling is something as small as giving into a child who demands their own way. It's sheltering a teen from natural consequences of inappropriate or destructive choices.

When kids are enabled to avoid pain, it's a coping mechanism. This can lead to unhealthy relationships and behavior.

Why do people enable?

An enabler doesn't like conflict, pain, disappointing others, or people being upset with them. They want to please people, including their child, at the expense of their own health, and the health of others. They avoid saying "no" because they don't want their child mad at them.

Perceptions of what's a "good" or "bad" mom, or making up for what was missed in childhood also influences a parent to enable.

Enabling feeds the dream that when everyone's happy, life is good.

Wanting kids to be exclusively happy isn't biblical. The only place in Scripture where everyone's happy is in the Garden of Eden—when Adam and Eve were sinless, in the full presence of God. Since then, adversity and pain have been part of the human experience.

Do you shy away from adversity? Do you make sure your children are happy, even when you know it's not best?

Could you be enabling your kids in small, yet significant ways?

Why They Need To Be Needy

Kids naturally resist pain. When you allow them to struggle, they'll test your limits, seeing if you will follow through on consequences. They'll whine, talk disrespectfully, or say, "You don't love me." Don't allow false guilt to lie to you. The truth is, when you love and support kids through their struggles, they know your love is unconditional.

They see you modeling God's relationship with His children. Instead of rescuing them from pain, you're with them all the way through it.

Your children need adversity so they'll need God; so they'll seek His help, comfort, and assistance. When *you* fill these needs, you steal opportunities for your child to learn God's power and comfort. Though it's hard to watch your kids struggle, they'll figure it out.

And they do, one way or another.

When in high school, one of my kids endured a difficult sports season that caused frustration and discouragement. Their self-confidence was depleted. Living in a small-knit, sports-centered community, individuals often asked me, "How is he doing?" and "Why doesn't he quit?" It was a situation where some kids may have quit from pressure and discouragement. However, persevering through that season made my son stronger. He returned the next year with more stamina, determination, and success.

Though it was tempting to rescue him by blaming or giving him the "okay" to quit, we saw strength arise within him. Had the struggle been taken away, he wouldn't have grown and changed.

Another time I watched a child struggle was when my daughter chose a college several states away. It caused her to seek God when we couldn't help her. Distance between you and your child is never easy. But trusting God and allowing your kids the opportunity to figure things out pays off. They gain independence, strength, and a greater dependence upon God.

Allowing struggle can be as little as making your child pick up the mess they made, or as big as helping them overcome an addiction. You can guide your children through adversity, or take the struggle away. Perseverance doesn't bring immediate happiness. But hard work, determination, and godly obedience brings confidence, contentment, and joy to your soul.

A Battle I Chose

When you're tempted to avoid confrontation with your kids, you're also at risk of enabling. Balancing life's craziness is easier without kids pushing boundaries, arguing, or disobeying. When they do this, you can either ignore the situation, or confront them. Choosing your battle is important. Certain behaviors are worth the struggle.

You're the gatekeeper of your child's soul. As a parent, you equip them with ethics, integrity, and faith for a lifetime. This won't come easily, because the enemy wants the heart of your child.

So the day Lil Wayne came to my house, it was a battle I was willing to fight.

It started when I saw the "explicit" icon beside iTunes songs purchased by my son. As the guardian of his soul, I routinely check what he puts in his mind and heart.

I Googled the song title. I read violent, sexualized, and degrading lyrics towards women by Lil Wayne. I was sick to my stomach.

At the time, I worked as a service provider for victims of domestic violence. My workday included real situations like those in the song. The lyrics were personal to me and those for whom I cared.

They weren't acceptable values in our home.

I knew a confrontation was inevitable when my son got home. I'd been through moments like this before—when it's easier to ignore behavior, avoid conflict, and pretend *it's not a big deal.*

Life's more peaceful when you let things slide.

But I'm accountable to God for what influences my child. So are you. The battle was non-negotiable. When my teen came home, the words flew as I predicted:

"You don't trust me."
"I'm seventeen! You don't need to monitor my music!"
"You're the only mom who makes a big deal out of stuff like this!"
"I hate you," was somewhere in the mix.

He stormed off. I was exhausted.

Parenting is hard work.

Over the next few days, Lil Wayne songs disappeared. New songs appeared. I checked the artists and lyrics, finding them acceptable. My teen found other rap artists whose messages were life-giving, not life-taking.

God won, Lil Wayne lost.

It was one of the last battles I fought for that boy's soul. In the aftermath, he wrote school assignments about the influence of music and how one artist, Lecrae, positively impacted him. Realizing how influential music is in his life, I learned that battle was worth fighting.

Even when it's uncomfortable or causes more stress in your life.

Reflection

Are you fearful about confronting your children? Do you wonder if you fall into the enablement trap? Take your thoughts and questions to God. Ask the Holy Spirit to show you where you might be enabling, even with young children.

Your children will suffer at some point, whether they're ten or forty. When you equip them to problem-solve, persevere, and have confidence in themselves, and God's presence in their lives, they'll be prepared when hard times come.

Where can you give your children space to struggle?

How can you allow them to learn perseverance, character, and new skills? Think of each child, and list areas for each one accordingly:

Father, give me patience and strength when I need to stand back and let my child struggle. Help me not to rescue, or enable, when you have a bigger and better plan for them. Equip me to encourage them in small moments, giving them confidence, without diminishing their capabilities to be successful. Help me to be honest with myself about my own fears or insecurities that cause me to rescue my child. Amen.

Twenty

You Are Important, Too

*"And my God will meet all of your needs according to
His glorious riches in Christ Jesus."*
PHILIPPIANS 4:19, NIV[34]

You need strength and perseverance just like your children—stamina for the not-so-easy-parenting moments. It's important to take care of yourself so you can choose your battles and guide your children through struggles.

As a mom, you naturally take care of others' needs first. Is taking care of yourself last on your list? Women are socialized to believe you're selfish if you take care of your needs before others. You may have even been told that.

Did you know God cares about you, your health, and your needs?

When you sacrifice your physical, emotional, or spiritual health, you can't give your best to the people you love. You also can't be the woman God's designed you to be.

You're too exhausted taking care of everyone else.

---

34 New International Version, biblegateway.com

Managing busyness doesn't mean taking self-care off the "to-do" list. Instead, you make it a priority.

Do you struggle doing this? Do you feel guilty or prideful if you take care of yourself?

If you breastfed, taking care of yourself was essential for the health of your child. It's equally essential for moms in other parenting stages to take care of themselves. Just as your baby needed you to rest so your milk could nurture her body, older children also need a healthy, rested mom to nurture their mental, spiritual, and emotional needs.

Do you feel rested? If not, ask yourself why? Is it from children getting up throughout the night? Is it from work related stress, a demanding child, or a strained marriage? Sleep is important for your body to take the demands of mothering, working, and all the activities in which you're involved. It's easy to rob yourself of sleep, so you can get more done after kids are in bed. Do you try to get one more thing accomplished while the house is quiet, when you have no one pulling on you, or asking for help?

Getting more sleep might involve changing your child's bedtime routine. If your child still gets up throughout the night, have you looked into possible reasons? You may want to talk to your doctor about what's normal for your child's age. Older children can have anxiety or fears causing interrupted sleep. If their physical and emotional wellbeing is okay, could you be enabling patterns that deprive sleep for both of you? You might need to practice the "don't steal the struggle" principle by letting them push through night time discomforts so you can both rest.

Perhaps you're getting sleep, but you're emotionally exhausted. If so, don't ignore those feelings. If whining kids or emotional teens drain you, take a time-out or have an evening away, so you can clear your head and have some space. Spend time with friends or family who uplift you, where you can be yourself, laugh, and feel like a person. If you can afford it, spend a night in a hotel where you can read, sleep, or relax at your leisure. I've periodically spent a night at a bed and breakfast during high-stress times when I've needed private space.

It's okay to take care of yourself.

If you're chronically tired, seek medical attention from a doctor or specialist. Excessive tiredness can be a symptom of serious physical conditions. However, if emotional or mental exhaustion is from marital, parenting, relationship, or work problems, don't ignore the situation. Don't minimize your feelings, the exhaustion, or the stress you're experiencing. Don't just assume your physical, mental, or emotional exhaustion is exclusively from parenting. Listen to your body's cues. Reach out for help when needed.

Busyness Isn't the Answer

For years, I was extremely busy. I ignored the fact that I was mentally and emotionally exhausted from parenting, working, and family conflict. Though I balanced external stresses well, internal turmoil came out in irritation, frustration, and anger. I needed physical, emotional, and spiritual rest. When I realized my condition was adversely affecting our family, I took control of what I could change.

I switched professions, worked on relationships, and prioritized self-care. I still work on balancing these things today.

You, too, can make life changes that positively impact your physical, mental, and emotional health. Don't put your needs last on the list. Prioritize your health needs for your current phase of parenting.

If your physical health is the issue, make an appointment with your physician. It's hard to fit exercise, good eating habits, and regular check-ups into an already busy schedule, but it's important. Prioritize what's needed the most. Snack on apples rather than a candy bar. Look for opportunities to exercise without making yourself busier. Instead of sitting while you wait for your child's practice to end, walk around the parking lot. Take the stroller out to calm a whiny toddler.

Whatever your needs are, don't ignore them.

Now that I'm forty-something, I realize prioritizing physical health is a lifetime investment. So is taking care of your mental and emotional health.

Have you ever wondered why God allows you to be a mom when you're young and don't have things together? I have.

Women bring hurts, insecurities, fears, and past relationships into motherhood. We bring coping skills, some of which may not be healthy. I began motherhood with an eating disorder. Being a parent challenged me to face the unhealthy behavior. When I decided I needed to change, it wasn't easy. Healthy replacement behavior didn't happen right away. I had to find different ways to cope with pain, emotions, and life.

Being a mom doesn't make your emotional wounds go away. In fact, pain from childhood experiences often surface while parenting your own kids. It's tempting to busy yourself so you don't have to face the whispers of your past. Don't ignore your hurt by making yourself more busy.

Busyness only masks the hurt inside of you.

If your emotional exhaustion is from toxic people or unhealthy situations, don't ignore the effect it's having on you. Acknowledge your needs. Talk to someone. It might be your spouse, friend, parent, or mentor. It also might require professional help through a physician, counselor, support group, or other trained professionals. Seeking professional help doesn't mean you're weak. It means you're strong. You will be stronger and healthier as you take care of yourself.

Self-care equips you to grow, flourish, and be the nurturer and daughter God desires you to be.

Even These Women Had Issues

It's easy to think other women have it all together, when you feel like you don't. If you've ever felt like that, you're not alone. Consider these biblical mothers who endured hard times:

Jochebed, mother of Moses, knew her child would be taken away and killed if he were found. She probably experienced fear, anger, and anxiety. Perhaps she felt depressed. But she responded with faith that God would take care of her and Moses, believing the Author of their story knew what He was doing (Exodus 1:2-10).

Hannah, mother of Samuel, was judged unfairly. Her pastor thought she was drunk. She was antagonized by her husband's other wife. Instead of responding in anger, she prayed fervently, pouring out her pain and grief to God. Instead of being offended by false accusations, she honestly said she was a deeply troubled woman (1 Samuel 1:15-16).

Mary, mother of Jesus, was misunderstood and judged with a pregnancy out of wedlock. Though she knew the truth about her pregnancy, she probably experienced gossip and judgment. Mary responded to her circumstances by clinging to the Lord when feeling alone and misjudged (Luke 1 & 2).

Sarah, mother of Isaac, was childless in old age when her husband had a child from another woman. She must have been jealous and bitter. Though she thought God had forgotten His promises, she gave birth to a son at age ninety (Genesis 12-23). Sarah witnessed God's faithfulness, even though she couldn't see it in the moment.

These women were just like you and me.

Their emotions and thoughts were similar to ones you and I have had. Have you ever thought:

Life isn't supposed to be this way.
This isn't what I expected.
Being a mom has more pain than joy.

Motherhood pain isn't a popular topic at church meetings or playgroups. Facebook, Instagram, and Twitter statuses rarely say, "Motherhood isn't what I bargained for – I don't think I can make it." If you're struggling, be encouraged from the lessons we learn from these women:

1. *They knew the Lord intimately.* Each of these mothers had a strong, personal faith in God. They knew His character was good even

when the situation said He wasn't. God is never absent from your situation or that of your children. He sees beyond the trial and knows the ending. You can take hope in that. When there's no hope in sight, you can look to the Author of your story.

2. *They clung to the Lord and His truth.* Clinging involves grabbing hold of, or refusing to let go. Despite their emotions, these women clung to the One they could have rejected. What do you cling to when life isn't what you signed up for? Do you hold onto a sovereign God, who sees the bigger picture? Do you stand in His truth when your emotions lead you astray? Your emotions betray you, but God never will.

3. *Motherhood didn't define their happiness.* Their relationship with God did. How did Mary get through the whispers and misunderstandings? How did Jochebed cope when her child was taken from her? Their happiness wasn't dependent on their dreams of motherhood. It was rooted in their relationship with the living God.

Encouragement for these moms didn't come from the culture around them. Their hope came from God, who was writing their story. If you've experienced similar feelings, be encouraged. The Bible includes real women in hard places, with real pain—in circumstances in which they didn't expect to find themselves. Places where there were no easy answers.

If you're a struggling mom, draw close to the God who gave these women strength.

Finding Wholeness

God created you to be whole so you can nurture His kingdom, in addition to your family. While managing busyness is important, the greater key to balancing life is finding wholeness.

What does it mean to be whole?

Being whole means you don't have gaping wounds in your mental and emotional make-up. It means you don't look to your children, husband, or others to meet your needs. It's facing your hurts and letting Jesus heal you, making you complete in His grace, love, and presence. How do you create wholeness?

The first step is giving up control. Give up control of your past, your pain, your insecurities, relationships, and unhealthy coping mechanisms. Give them to Jesus, the Comforter, Savior, and Redeemer. As you hand these areas to God, Christ will take over. He creates a wholeness that balances out the unevenness in your life. Seeking help or support from people you trust puts action to your faith, believing that God will provide for your needs in significant ways (Philippians 4:19).

The second step is letting Jesus fill the gaps of your life. When you release control to Jesus, you allow yourself to be filled up by Him. As you pray, apply His Word, and let Him complete your lesser-strengths, you'll receive the peace of mind only God provides (Philippians 4:6-7). It's tempting to think other things will make you happy and whole. They won't. Let Jesus supply all of your needs according to His glorious riches in Him (Philippians 4:19)!

The third step is obeying what God asks you to do. Obey God first before doing what others tell you to do. God is the Head of your life. If your spouse, parent, child, boss, or co-worker asks you to do something in direct disobedience to God, obey God, not man. When in doubt, God is the one you need to obey (Luke 11:28).

When you're grounded in Christ, you worry less about what others think of you. You find balance in Him, and His will for your life.

People will fail you, but God never will.

Finding Balance

If you don't have physical or emotional wounds, it's still important to take care of yourself. Take time to not be a mom for a few hours. It's refreshing.

Another self-care principle from earlier chapters is releasing expectations. It's a life principle that creates balance. Take your strengths and lesser-strengths seriously. Release expectations of what you think you need to be or do. Get rid of the Supermom image. Be comfortable with yourself. Seek God, first, for His expectations of you. Let these principles guide your self-care.

Lastly, beware of multitasking. Though multitasking balances responsibilities, there's danger when you do too much, and don't rest your mind or spirit. You can be so efficient getting things done, your mind doesn't shut off.

Your brain needs rest!

Remember when God convicted me that running was out of balance? He also revealed how multitasking was out of control. It was another defining moment for me.

It happened one summer when I visited my sister and couldn't sleep. She was a single mom with young kids. Instead of lying in bed, I got up to see what I could do to help her. I started out folding laundry, then washed walls. I washed the curtains on her stairway windows. The middle-of-the-night cleaning escapade resulted in pulling the curtains out of the dryer, only to find holes in them from the dryer heat.

I was caught.

God showed me how out of balance I was. As a guest in someone's home, I couldn't even be still without finding something to do.

I realized I didn't know how to rest. Multitasking had become the first response to silent moments.

It wasn't healthy. It was a wake-up call to the level of busyness and stress in which I lived. I was convicted that I needed to be still and rest.

That's what God desires of you. He wants you to be still and rest in health and peace.

⟋

Reflection

Taking care of yourself is one of the most important parts of balance. What are your current physical, emotional, or spiritual needs?

What is the immediate area in which you need to practice self-care?

If you need help implementing self-care, who can you reach out to—your husband? A friend? A mentor or counselor?

Choose one area of self-care and do something for yourself today. Then repeat it and make it part of a balanced lifestyle.

⟋

Father, help me to see where I need to take care of myself. Remove the lies that say I'm prideful or selfish if I practice self-care. Show me where I need to rest and heal. Thank you for caring about me. Amen.

Twenty-One

The Love Affair That's Not With Your Husband

"Only one thing is essential and Mary has chosen it."
LUKE 10:38-42, THE MESSAGE[35]

*Y*ou can implement every tool in this book for better life balance. But if you don't make your relationship with Jesus a priority, your efforts are in vain.

When you miss time with Jesus, you miss the most important thing.

Satan lies to you. He'll make you wonder how you can add one more thing, like time with Jesus, to your day. He'll distract you by the "how-to's" for balancing life. He'll want you to focus on getting that closet organized or those freezer meals cooked right now, instead of spending time in God's Word or prayer.

Making Jesus your first priority creates a dilemma. How can you spend time with Him and take care of work, family, and home? I'm thankful Jesus understands immediate demands and the struggle to do what's important. He even includes an example in Scripture. Among

---

35 The Message, bibiegateway.com

Jesus' closest friends were women who battled between busyness and making time for what's important.

Jesus had two friends, Mary and Martha, who were sisters. One day, Martha invited Jesus to her home. While He was there, her sister, Mary, was listening to Jesus while sitting at His feet. Scripture reports Martha was distracted by all the preparations to be made. Can you identify with her distractions? I sure can.

This was their dialogue:

"She came to him and asked, 'Lord, don't you care that my sister has left me to do the work by myself? Tell her to help me out!' 'Martha, Martha,' the Lord answered. 'You are worried and upset about many things, but only one thing is needed. Mary has chosen what is better and it will not be taken from her.'" Luke 10:40b-42 (NIV)[36]

Can you hear yourself in the conversation? Do immediate needs cause you to miss opportunities to be with Jesus?

Do you live like Martha, but long to be like Mary?

Worship Gets the Laundry Done

When you get frustrated because you can't do it all, hear Jesus' voice; *My daughter, only one thing is needed right now—worship Me.*

I'll be honest, sometimes I think, "Worship doesn't get the laundry done, the kids picked up, or deadlines met!" Or does it?

Bringing God's presence into your life creates balance in your busyness.

Time with God doesn't have to be formal. As a busy mom with unavoidable responsibilities, finding ways to intimately connect with God is important. It's personal. What works for you may not work for another mom. You might have to be creative and unconventional. When

---

36 New International Version, biblegateway.com

Mary sat down at Jesus' feet, she was being unconventional. Yet, it met her needs.

What are your needs for time with Jesus?

Share your needs with God. His peace passes all understanding (Philippians 4:6-7). When you come to Him as Mary did, you receive His peace and calm even if you're busier than you'd like to be.

I've spent most of my life caught in the trap between building my relationship with God and the demands of what I think needs to be done *now*. The good-Christian-woman image says you're supposed to be immersed in God's Word, yet also be fastidious serving at home, church, and community. Being hospitable, volunteering, leading Bible studies, managing a well-run home, providing great meals, having a robust devotional time, on top of parenting, being a wife, and working—these are the unwritten rules about who a godly woman should be.

The list is exhausting. No wonder Martha was irritable and frustrated. I can relate with her, can you?

You have limited resources to do everything that commands your time and attention. When you constantly meet the immediate demands around you, you miss opportunities to develop an intimate relationship with your heavenly Father. Those immediate demands never go away.

Only one thing is essential, says Jesus—sitting and listening to the Father.

Finding the balance between being Mary and Martha-like in your relationship with God is the hidden key to managing responsibilities. It doesn't matter what stage of life you're in, or whether you're married, or a single mom. Being a parent takes time and energy. Making time for your relationship with God is essential to meet the physical, mental, and emotional demands of parenting.

When your kids are young, they take more of your physical energy. As they grow through the teen and young adult years, parenting takes more of your emotional and mental energy. And it doesn't stop when they go to college or move out on their own. Instead, your emotional and spiritual needs change. You move from being the "fixer," to "coach," then "intercessor,"taking your child's situations and those of your grandchildren to the Father in prayer.

In all of these roles, it's essential to sit and listen to the Father.

Developing a Mary-Like Lifestyle

Don't wait until your kids get older, or when life slows down to develop an intimate relationship with God. Each parenting stage brings different challenges. Prioritizing your time with God *now* helps all aspects of life. Without that intimate relationship, you get caught up in the day-to-day demands, developing a Martha-like demeanor:

Complaining (Why isn't anyone helping me?)
Self-pity (Don't you care?)
Distracted (But, I've got to get this done!)
Demanding (Tell her to help me!)

Does that sound like you? I've been that way plenty of times. When you don't prioritize time with Jesus, these feelings quickly rise to the surface, driving your attitudes, actions, and responsibilities. It becomes harder to hear Him, to gain His perspective, and priorities. It's harder to receive His peace and calm.

Time with the Savior balances all other activities and attitudes of the heart.

How do you find time to cultivate that relationship? Like every other principle we've talked about, it starts with releasing your expectations of an ideal time with God.

Making It Personal

Don't rely on Sunday mornings or yearly retreats to fill you with God's presence. You need consistent, frequent communication with the Father to receive the fullness of His peaceful presence and perspective. Intimacy with Jesus needs priority and time, just like human relationships.

When I was a new mom, I thought godly women got up early, every day, to spend time with Jesus. Though I often tried it, I usually failed. I'm not an early riser. That expectation brought frustration and self-condemnation. Even though I made time with Jesus during the children's afternoon nap, I still felt I was falling short.

Have you had similar expectations?

Since we're letting go of ideals and expectations, let's release that Superwoman image.

Though it's a good discipline to get up early for worship and Bible study, it's not for everyone. Instead, find a time that works for you. Like other priorities, you may need to be creative.

If you're a stay-at-home mom, a devotional time might be during your children's naps. If your kids don't nap regularly, it might be in 15-20 minute intervals, several times a week while your kids are playing or watching a movie. Find a corner for a few minutes where you can be alone to read the Bible, pray, and praise.

If you're working outside of the home, driving time to or from work can be your prayer time. Turn off the radio and be quiet before God. Or, listen to audio readings of the Bible on your phone or iPod rather than listening to music. I also try to get to work a few minutes early to have devotions at my desk. Having five to ten minutes to read or journal quiets my heart for the workday, centering my attitudes and actions on God, rather than absorbing the perspectives of a secular environment.

Making time with God is feasible when you use pockets of time. Do you look at social media first thing each morning? Instead, spend time in His Word. If you're waiting at a child's practice or at the doctor's office, use that time to read your Bible, journal, or pray. If you exercise, use a Bible app to read or listen to. Talk to God through prayer, or praise Him for His attributes. At the end of the day when the kids are in bed, instead of picking up one more toy or doing another load of laundry, take a few minutes to journal, processing your day with God.

You have many moments in your day to spend with Jesus. Can you use your time on social media or watching TV to talk to God instead?

He wants time with you. "Come near to God and He will come near to you," James 4:8, NIV.[37]

How are you investing your time?

Whatever time you give God, be intentional, be present, and consistent. Find what works best for you, then do it.

Just You and Him

When I teach about this principle to women's groups, a common question is, "How do you study the Bible on your own?"

The best way to know your heavenly Father is by listening to Him through His Word. The Bible is God's love letter to you. While group and individual Bible studies are good, reading someone else's perspective about God, even from this book, doesn't replace the truth of His Word. Scripture reveals God's character, and declares His promises. It contains lessons and applications that are personal to you.

In my own journey, God's Word gave strength and power to overcome an eating disorder. When I experienced grief and depression, it gave hope and perspective. It continually convicts me of sin and wrongful attitudes. It's my lifeline when circumstances tell me God isn't good.

The Bible reveals God's character and perspective. Through Scripture, you see Him interact with people who have real emotions, thoughts, and circumstances like yours. He becomes personal to you, One with whom you have a close, intimate relationship.

"I, the Lord, do not change" God says in Malachi 3:6 (NIV).[38]

Since God doesn't change, His truth and promises in Scripture don't change. The more you know God through His Word, the more you understand His grace, abundant love, and permanent character.

---

37 New International Version, biblegateway.com
38 New International Version, biblegateway.com

"Blessed is the one…whose delight is in the law of the Lord, and who meditates on His law day and night. That person is like a tree planted by streams of water, which yields fruit in season and whose leaf does not wither—whatever they do prospers" Psalm 1:1a, 2-3 (NIV).[39]

Like a tree whose roots grow deep, when you're grounded in God's Word, you're prepared when adversity hits. You're empowered by the Holy Spirit to live the priorities you're trying to balance. Instead of completing more "to-do" lists, spending time in His Word allows you to soak up His peace and perspective for daily demands.

Like Mary, it places you at His feet, listening to the Father, and receiving His grace.

The Love Affair That's Not With My Husband

Nothing satisfies like the Word of the Living God. In times of peace, it nourishes and strengthens. In times of pain, it heals and gives hope. In times of drought, it brings life.

My love affair with the Bible started as a teenager. At fifteen, a modern translation I read made God personal when I felt no one understood me. At seventeen, His Word became alive when I overcame temptation in my eating disorder. God provided a way out of a tempting situation, just like He promises in 1 Corinthians 10:13.

As a college student, I gave up sin in which I was living because His Word convicted me. While everything was permissible, not everything was beneficial (1 Corinthians 10:23).

As a young mom with postpartum depression, I learned God cared about the struggle to just get through the day (Psalm 142). When I experienced grief, the Bible said God saw my tears, and recorded each of them (Psalm 56:8).

---

39 New International Version, biblegateway.com

In preparation to go back to the workforce when my children were young, His Word assured me that God would supply all of our needs according to His glorious riches in Christ Jesus (Philippians 4:19).

As a parent struggling with anger and frustration, God repeatedly promised He would repay the years the locusts have eaten (Joel 2:25). When reading scripture to a friend dying of a brain tumor, His word was a balm to her body as she accepted Christ as Savior in the bed of a nursing home.

From these situations, and others, I've developed a love affair with God and His Word. He's shown me Scripture is applicable to your life.

Always.

Making It Personal

Even if you have only a few minutes to read a passage of Scripture, there are a variety of ways to study the Bible so it's personal. First, start with a book of the Bible that's interesting or easy to read. Any of the gospels (Matthew, Mark, Luke, or John), James, 1 John, Galatians, Ephesians, Philippians, Colossians, I & 2 Timothy, or 1 & 2 Peter are easier books in the New Testament to study. In the Old Testament, the Psalms, Proverbs, Esther, or Ruth are interesting places to start.

When reading a passage of Scripture, make personal connections with the text. Questions you can ask yourself when reading a passage include:

What does this passage tell me about God's character? No matter whether it's an Old Testament story, a prophetic book, or a New Testament passage, you learn something about God's character from Scripture. Try keeping a list of God's attributes in a journal or notepad with corresponding verses listed beside each attribute. You can use the list when you need to be reminded about God's character. (He's patient, strong, full of grace, etc.).

136

What can I learn from people in the story? The amazing thing about the Bible is that it's God's story of history. No matter what's happening in the passage, there are many perspectives involved. When reading a portion of Scripture, look at what's going on from the person's experience in the story. What do you see or not see? What would the experience be like if you were in the story? What lessons are the people learning from their experience or interaction with God, Jesus, or the Holy Spirit?

What is God's perspective in the passage? James 1:5 says, "If any of you lacks wisdom, you should ask God, who gives generously to all without finding fault, and it will be given to you" (NIV). Matthew 7:7 says, "Ask and it will be given to you; seek and you will find; knock and the door will be opened to you" (NIV).[40] There's another perspective to the Bible, and that's God's perspective. He's the Author of Scripture. He'll give you wisdom and perspective when you ask Him. What does God see, being omniscient and omnipresent, that people in the story can't see? Where is God in their experience? When you ask God what His perspective is, the Holy Spirit will reveal it to you. When you read Scripture through God's perspective, not only will the Bible become more alive, you'll begin seeing your life through His perspective, too.

What's a life lesson I can learn from this passage? When I taught U.S. History, I required students to find applicable principles from the historical context. They did. Finding life lessons gave them a different perspective of history. It's the same with the Bible; it's His story (like history). Every word is ordained by the sovereign, living God. He desires to teach truths we can apply to our lives. You can learn something from any passage of Scripture.

---

40 New International Version, biblegateway.com

What can I apply to my life from this passage? It's one thing to be inspired by Scripture, but it takes action to apply a lesson, conviction, or principle to your life. After looking at God's character, perspective, or facts you've learned through Scripture, respond to it. How does God's character affect your understanding of Him? How can you apply His perspective to your situation? How can you change your response to an attitude, struggle, or current circumstance?

What is praise-worthy in this passage? What promises, truths, or perspectives do you see in the passage for which you can praise God? How can you praise God for the application of His Word to your situation? What hope do you receive from Scripture for which you can thank Him?

God's word isn't a mystical, ancient piece of literature, it's"...*living and active, sharper than any double-edged sword, it penetrates even to dividing soul and spirit, joints and marrow; it judges the thoughts and attitudes of the heart.*" Hebrews 4:12, NIV.[41]

The more time you spend in Scripture, the more intimate you'll be with your Creator. His peace will encompass you, bringing balance, perspective, and wholeness to the various roles you fill.

Building Relationships

Intimacy with God isn't complete by just reading the Bible. When Mary sat at Jesus' feet, she did more than just listen and talk with Him. She studied His face, observed His mannerisms, and watched His interactions with others. She was close enough to hear a soft whisper He might share with those around Him that no one else could hear.

She was vulnerable in His presence, regardless of what people thought of her.

That's an intimate relationship.

---

41 New International Version, biblegateway.com

While you don't have physical proximity with Jesus, you can have a similar closeness. In addition to Bible study, how do you build a closer relationship with Jesus?

First, pray God's Word. Scripture is God's heart and voice to us. Praying Scripture brings strength, power, and courage to a stressed and weary mind. Praying God's Word for yourself, your children, and others is powerful, life giving, and releases authority in the spiritual realm where the enemy is present. Praying Scripture brings His will upon the petitions you are bringing Him.

Second, worship God. God created us to glorify and worship Him. When we worship God in spirit and truth, we please Him, and He draws close to us. He provides peace and balance in the moment, no matter where you are. Worship takes your focus off yourself and your circumstances, and brings you to the feet of Jesus. Worship can be done anywhere—while folding laundry, driving to preschool, or on the way home from Walmart. Find ways God speaks to you through words, or songs, in your busyness.

As you spend time with God, your busyness will be more balanced. What can you do today to become more intimate with Jesus?

Prioritizing God's Word as a Family

"Impress them upon your children...write them on the door-frames of your house" Deuteronomy 6:7a, 9a (NIV).[42]

Does your image of family devotions include well-behaved kids sitting around a table, intently listening to Father reading from the Bible? Like an iconic family picture, Norman Rockwell style?

When my husband and I first attempted family devotions, we had children from middle school to preschool age. We wanted active listening, attentive answers, and expected them to sit still. Instead, the

---

42 New International Version, biblegateway.com

younger kids rolled on the floor, didn't want to answer questions, and the teenager said, "This is lame." We only did it a few times before we stopped.

Sound familiar?

Having high expectations for corporate devotions sets a family up for failure. After hearing suggestions about a family worship time at a Christian family camp, my husband and I revamped our expectations and practices of family devotions. Instead of it being a structured, formal setting, it's a time where we gather, once a week, for ten or fifteen minutes. We share things for which we're thankful, and things we're learning from God. We talk about our week. Sometimes there's Bible trivia. We sing a few Sunday school songs or choruses, though painfully off-key.

We always pray.

Sometimes, in our busyness and teenagers' schedules, praying for our week is the only thing we do. But we do it, every week.

The consistency of simple, family devotions has created an openness in our family we've relied on during hard times. Praying, sharing with each other, and being unified has been powerful when things have rocked our world.

A family does business with the enemy when united in His presence.

The most important principle for devotions is to find what works for your family, then do it. Consistently. Over the years of having family worship time, here are a few principles we've learned about family time with God:

Whatever format you choose, be consistent. Family devotions don't need to be perfect, but when they're consistent, they're important to your family's routine.

Your kids need to hear God's Word at home. There's something remarkable about reading the Word of God together in a home where it's honored.

In a fast-paced life, gathering as a family is important. As your kids get older, it's harder to get your family all together. Gathering together other than at mealtime is impactful. For a few minutes, you're connected and not distracted by food, TV, cell phones, or social media. You talk, listen, and engage.

Gathering together strengthens family bonds. In families with multiple children, or an age gap between siblings, opportunities to interact build life-long connections between siblings. Family worship time and prayer has strengthened our family identity.

Praying together is powerful. Corporate devotions allow us to pray boldly for each other when we otherwise wouldn't—praying about serious issues rather than ignoring them. The enemy wants to steal and destroy God's plan for your children. Corporate prayer is powerful for declaring God's victory and presence in your home. We've also prayed blessings over our children, one by one, declaring God's grace and favor over their lives. There's power when a family prays blessings together over each and every member.

Our family worship times aren't perfect. They've included grumbling children who mumble under their breath. However, kids really do listen, even if you don't think they do. Don't give up—resistance is natural!

What are more ideas for a family worship time?

- *Read a brief passage of Scripture* with a short lesson.
- *Sing a hymn or praise song.* Take turns letting your kids pick the song.
- *Pray for each other.* Have everyone pray for the person on their left or right. (It's powerful to hear siblings who don't get along pray for each other.)
- *Do Bible trivia.*

- *Pose a question*: What was the highlight of your week? Where did you see God work? If you could ask Mom or Dad any question, what would it be? Be creative, or keep it simple.
- *Make family worship time short*—10 to 15 minutes. Even if you only have few minutes, at least pray together.

The focus of family devotions should be simple, consistent, and Christ-centered. Keeping those factors in mind, don't put it off. Start today. It'll create important memories for your family during the years your children are home.

⌒⌐

Reflection

What obstacles have kept you from reading the Bible?

What suggestions from this chapter might work for you?

What part of your day or routine can you use to have a quiet time with God?

How can you start implementing a Christ-centered family time?

Father, thank you that your Word is true, that it's Your love letter to me. Thank you that it fully equips me for every need in my life, from the practical tasks of the day to the my deepest hurt or that of my child. Help me to know You through your Word, that my roots will grow deep to receive your truth for balance and peace. Show me your character, your perspective, and lessons I can apply to my life. Amen.

Twenty-Two

BEING OBEDIENT AND LEAVING
THE RESULTS TO GOD

Trust and obey, for there's no other way.

As we get to the finale of balance, busyness, and not doing it all, there's one area we can't ignore. It's a silent tactic the enemy uses to snatch priorities and drive unnecessary busyness: It's fear.

Fear your kids won't turn out right,
      …that your failures will harm them.
Fear they won't get along with their siblings,
      …that they won't be successful.
Fear that bad things will come to your family,
      …that your children will hate you.
Fear your child's failure will define you,
      …that they won't have a relationship with Christ.
Fear that your family dream won't come true.

These fears are real. We live in a fallen world where sin, depravity, and humanity encompass the best and worst of life. None of us knows

144

what the future for our family, marriage, or children will be. Fear of the unknown keeps a lot of parents bound to skewed and unbalanced priorities. Things scream for your attention and material investments. There's so much for which to strive. Things which steal time and energy from what's eternal.

One story in Scripture shares a real couple's experience with fear, doubt, promise, and belief. If you're a parent who fears the unknown, you can learn a lot from the parents in this story—Abraham and Sarah.

Let's look at their story in Genesis 12-23, finding applications you can directly apply to your life.

Sarah's Disbelief

From the beginning of their story, God promises outlandish things to Abraham and Sarah. He says they'll have offspring that will outnumber the grains of sand. He says that Sarah, old and barren, will birth a nation.

A hopeful promise to a woman whose dreams weren't realized. What a cruel joke Sarah must have thought God was playing on her.

But in the midst of her pain as a childless woman, God saw her. Genesis 11:30 says, "Sarah was barren, she had no children" (NASB).[43] This simple sentence with a double emphasis tells the reader that God knew and saw her suffering. God could have just said she was barren. It would have been enough to explain her condition. But He noted, again, "She had no children."

In her pain, I wonder if Sarah felt forgotten; if she wondered where God was. The double emphasis of her condition tells you God had not forgotten her.

God saw Sarah's situation and knew her agony.

However, Sarah responded in disbelief. She didn't believe God was going to do what He said He would. Instead of faithfully waiting for

---

43 New American Standard Version, bible gateway.com

the promised pregnancy, Sarah hurried God's plan along. Sarah had her husband, Abraham, have sexual relations with her servant, Hagar, so she could have her son, according to custom. Fathering a child by another woman brought strife, jealousy, and conflict to their home. Sarah later regretted the decision. She despised Hagar and hated the son her servant bore.

That conflict still continues today. According to religious custom, Hagar's son, Ishmael, is the father of Palestine, and Isaac is the father of Israel.

What a mess.

Have you ever been impatient with God's promises for your family and took things into your own hands? How did it turn out? While God can work through mistakes, there are natural consequences when you short-change His plans. There's often heartache and angst when you work outside of God's will (Genesis 16, Genesis 21).

If you've taken things into your own hands, like Sarah, you're not alone. Too many times I've been impatient and moved God's plans along. Each time, there was some kind of emotional duress.

I've learned the hard way that it's best to obey God. Every time.

The Trap of Doubt and Disbelief

The Bible doesn't record much dialog between God and Sarah. But the conversation it does record includes laughter and lies. After Hagar's son, Ishmael, was born, God spoke to Abraham through three visitors who proclaimed Sarah would give birth at ninety years of age. Overhearing the promise, Sarah laughed at God:

"*After I am worn out and my master is old, will I now have this plea-sure?' She thought to herself*" (Genesis 18:12, NIV).[44] Can't you hear the doubt and questions in her mind?

God answered Abraham instead of Sarah, "Why did Sarah laugh and say, 'Will I really have a child, now that I am old?' Is anything too

---

44 New International Version, biblegateway.com

hard for the Lord? I will return to you at the appointed time next year and Sarah will have a son" (Genesis 18:13-14, NIV).[45]

Sarah was afraid because God knew she laughed. She lied to God by saying, "I did not laugh." He responded, "Yes, you did laugh" (Genesis 18:15, NIV).[46]

Oops. You can't hide anything from God.

Do you see yourself in Sarah? When circumstances don't look promising, do you sarcastically laugh at and question God? Instead of asking God honest questions, like "I don't understand," do you mock your heavenly Father? Do you get stuck in doubt, rather than walk in belief?

A lot of women fall into this trap. Though you have a personal relationship with Jesus Christ, you fail to trust Him for His goodness, His promises, and for the future of your family. You doubt God's ability to fulfill His promises rather than believing in His character. You fail to have faith in the unseen.

I've done this. Have you?

Sarah couldn't get past the reality of her circumstances. Instead of receiving the promise and praising God (Luke 1:46-55), she responded in disbelief. Unlike Elizabeth, who was also promised a child in old age, she lacked assurance. Elizabeth responded to her promise by saying, *"Blessed is she who has believed that the Lord would fulfill His promise to her!"* (Luke 1:45, NIV).[47]

Sarah laughed, instead.

Even when the miracle child, Isaac, was born, Sarah said, "God has brought me laughter and everyone who hears about this will laugh with me…Who would have said to Abraham that Sarah would nurse children? Yet I have borne him a son in his old age" (Genesis 21:6-7, NIV).[48]

---

45 New International Version, biblegateway.com
46 New International Version, biblegateway.com
47 New International Version, biblegateway.com
48 New International Version, biblegateway.com

While Sarah's laughter may have included joy, there's still a hint of disbelief in her voice; *Who would have believed that I would nurse children?*

That would be God, Sarah. God told Abraham you would nurse children.

But you didn't believe.

That is her sin.

Taking God at His word requires obedient faith. It means you believe He hasn't forgotten you when your emotions say differently. It's waiting for Him, rather than taking things into your own hands when you don't see your prayers answered. It's trusting God is who He says He is, that His power is real—that He has goodness in store when the circumstances seem hopeless.

Abraham's Obedience

Though Sarah models disbelief, Abraham inspires radical faith. When God told Abraham to offer his son as a sacrifice of worship, he obeyed. He loaded his donkey, took some firewood, two servants, and began a three-day journey with Isaac to Mount Moriah. When they approached the mountain, he told his servants to hang back—he and Isaac were going to worship on the mountain. Then, he told the servants he and the boy would be back. Genesis 22:6-19 (NIV)[49] tells the rest of the story:

Abraham took the wood for the burnt offering and placed it on his son Isaac, and he himself carried the fire and the knife. As the two of them went on together, Isaac spoke up and said to his father Abraham, "Father?"

"Yes, my son?" Abraham replied.

"The fire and wood are here," Isaac said, "but where is the lamb for the burnt offering?"

---

49 New International Version, biblegateway.com

Abraham answered, "God himself will provide the lamb for the burnt offering, my son." And the two of them went on together.

When they reached the place God had told him about, Abraham built an altar there and arranged the wood on it. He bound his son Isaac and laid him on the altar, on top of the wood. Then he reached out his hand and took the knife to slay his son. But the angel of the Lord called out to him from heaven, "Abraham! Abraham!"

"Here I am," he replied.

"Do not lay a hand on the boy," he said. "Do not do anything to him. Now I know that you fear God, because you have not withheld from me your son, your only son."

Abraham looked up and there in a thicket he saw a ram caught by its horns. He went over and took the ram and sacrificed it as a burnt offering instead of his son.

So Abraham called that place The Lord Will Provide. And to this day it is said, "On the mountain of the Lord it will be provided."

The angel of the Lord called to Abraham from heaven a second time and said, "I swear by myself, declares the Lord, that because you have done this and have not withheld your son, your only son, I will surely bless you and make your descendants as numerous as the stars in the sky and as the sand on the seashore. Your descendants will take possession of the cities of their enemies, and through your offspring all nations on earth will be blessed, because you have obeyed me."

Then Abraham returned to his servants, and they set off together for Beersheba. And Abraham stayed in Beersheba. Genesis 22:6-19 (NIV)[50]

Can't you image Abraham's initial questions he asked of God:

Really, God? You finally give me the promised son after all of these years. You told me his descendants will number as far as the eye can see. You want me to sacrifice him as an offering to You?

What kind of sick joke is this?

---

50 New International Version, biblegateway.com

Even if Abraham didn't have those questions, would you? I would. As a parent, this story deeply effects me. Through Abraham's obedience, I learn about complete faith in God's provisions for my children. It's the perfect example of obedient faith. When it didn't make sense, Abraham obeyed God wholeheartedly.

Then, he trusted God for the results.

When Isaac asked Abraham where the lamb was for the burnt offering, Abraham unswervingly responded: "God himself will provide a lamb for the burnt offering, my son" (Genesis 22:8, NIV).[51]

Abraham's response gives me hope as I intercede for my kids. Like him, I need to faithfully respond by obediently trusting God will provide for my child.

For your child.

This is what God wants from you as a parent: Instead of being busy doing good things, obediently trust Him for your child's life. Follow Him without taking things into your own hands. Hope in God's goodness and plan.

Believe that God, Himself, will provide.

Why Obedience Brings Balance

Abraham probably had the same fears for Isaac as you have for your children. Behind his stoic answers of obedience, was he afraid of the unknowns up the mountain? It's natural to fearfully respond to what's ahead. In a fast-paced culture, fears drive parents to ensure a positive outcome for their kids. With pressures to make your kids popular, accepted, or successful, fears drive distracted priorities. Even in the Christian culture, you believe messages that being a "good parent" means getting your kids into the right programs or making them live a certain way. You fearfully get busy doing what everyone else is doing, rather than obeying God and trusting Him for the results of your child's future.

---

51   New International Version, biblegateway.com

You submit to the world instead of yielding to God.

That's why your relationship with God is essential for establishing priorities and managing busyness. You're a life-giver in a generation where God is mocked. Raising children who love God requires obedience to walk where God leads you. Like Abraham, it requires deep faith, honest obedience, and diligence to believe what you can't see.

It's believing God, Himself, will provide.

Balanced parenting isn't striving to guarantee the future you hope for your kids. It's sacrificial obedience modeled by Abraham; leaving your fears and control on the altar of Christ. It's continually offering your child and their future to God, doing what He's called you to do, and leaving the results to Him.

It's laying your child before Jesus, no matter what, trusting God will provide.

It's not easy. Over and over, I have to faithfully obey God with my child's circumstances when I don't know the outcome. Every time I do it, my trust in God deepens.

I've learned obedience to God is better than short-changing His will because of impatience, fear, or pride.

"Blessed is she who has believed that the Lord would fulfill His promises to her" Luke 1:45 (NIV).[52]

Reflection

What fears about your child's future drive your priorities or busyness?

---

52 New International Version, biblegateway.com

In what situations have you taken things in your own hands instead of allowing God to work?

What was the outcome?

How can you boldly obey God, believing He, Himself, will provide?

⁓

Father, I need faith that You will provide. Holy Spirit, build this faith in me. Equip me to walk in Your steps when I can't see the road ahead of me. Draw me to obedience when my emotions want to doubt, saying, "God really said that?" Empower me to walk in Your strength in obedient faith. Thank you that You will provide. Amen.

Twenty-Three

PRAYERS OF FAITH

⌐◞

*"Do not be anxious about anything, but in every
situation, by prayer and petition, with thanksgiving,
present your requests to God. And the peace of God,
which transcends all understanding, will guard
your hearts and your minds in Christ Jesus."*

PHILIPPIANS 4:6-7 NIV[53]

*H*ere we are. The final chapter of how to live a balanced life in
the midst of busyness. The principles aren't textbook answers
from a professional who's removed from the struggle of parenting,
busyness, and balance. I'm right beside you, practicing these principles,
making daily choices about time, priorities, and expectations. In fact,
while writing this book, busyness crept in at an alarming rate. New
challenges, both professional and personal, came my way.

This book is as much for me as it is for you.

Which brings me to the last principle—the significance of prayer.
As my kids face new challenges, I'm learning how prayers of bold faith
bring peace. They keep you from being distracted by fears, insecurities,

---

53 New International Version, biblegateway.com

and life's demands. Intimate prayer reminds me how God cares about every aspect of our lives, and that of our families.

I've been guilty of thinking God is removed from diapers, sporting events, carpooling, and college visits. He's not.

Philippians 4:6-7 is a prayer for moms overwhelmed by details, deadlines, dirt, and despair.

"Do not be anxious about anything, but in every situation, by prayer and petition, with thanksgiving, present your requests to God. And the peace of God, which transcends all understanding, will guard your heart and mind in Christ Jesus" Philippians 4:6-7, NIV.[54]

This verse commands us not to be anxious about *anything*. Instead, bring *everything* to the Father in prayer. With *thanksgiving*. When you do this, God promises His peace, which transcends all understanding, will guard your heart and mind in Christ Jesus.

Do you need a peace that passes all understanding?

I do. Recently, I needed peace like I never before needed.

Each word in Scripture is intentional and significant. When Paul, the author of Philippians, says to bring *everything* in prayer, he means it. So does God.

The more I practice this discipline, the more I realize God really means *all* and *everything*. In the simplest and most difficult moments, He truly supplies a peace that passes all understanding.

God cares about your daily struggles, your decisions to prioritize, and your desire to find balance.

He cares when you take off work for a sick child. He cares about the fight you just had with your teenager, and the tantrum your seven-year-old just had. Every part of your life, and that of your child, is important to Him. When you present all your requests to Jesus, trusting Him for results, you'll be more peaceful.

You'll learn to trust Him, let go of expectations, and be free.

---

54 New International Version, biblegateway.com

Practical Prayer

The great thing about prayer is it can happen anywhere. You can pray while driving, waiting for a child's practice to end, or before you start your work day. Prayer can be an attitude of gratitude that follows you wherever you go. Praise filled prayer transforms your thinking about a situation. It changes your feelings from negative to positive. It focuses your perspective on Christ and what's eternally important, instead of what's immediate and temporal.

When it's hard to thank God for difficult circumstances, focus your praise on God's character, lessons you're learning from Scripture, or blessings from obedience. When you thank God for His attributes, He draws your attention away from self, discouragement, or worry. Your heart and mind refocuses on God's truth. Embracing God's perspective renews your mind (Romans 12:1-2). Then, you're able to receive His unfathomable peace.

Other significant prayers are speaking blessings over your children. When you pray blessings over your family and their circumstances, God releases His favor and goodness in situations. When you don't know how to pray for your kids, praying God's blessing on them releases God's will to be done.

Asking God's blessing doesn't guarantee things will turn out the way you want them. It means God will provide the longings of His heart, not yours.

It's something greater than you can ask or imagine for your situation.

God's calling you and I to bring *everything* to Him by petition. Everything includes situations out of your control, people's behaviors you can't predict, and every small detail of which you panic or worry.

When heartache floods my emotions, He's teaching me to sit at His feet, like Mary, instead of complaining and telling Him what to do. When I come to Him and pour out my heart, longings, and fears, I trust His character by faith.

God continually shows Himself true and faithful in hard situations. He gives a peace that passes all understanding, guarding your heart and mind in Christ Jesus.

Praying Scripture

Praying Scripture is powerful. When you pray Scripture for a situation or person, you're literally praying God's Word and desires back to Him. You release the power of God's Word for the situation. You become confident when praying—His words sink down deep inside of you. Scriptural prayers provide truth and perspective for balancing priorities, because it defines *His* priorities.

Praying Scripture releases the fullness of God's power on earth, and in heaven.

There's one prayer I pray for moms to whom I minister. It's one I've prayed for you as I've written this book. It's what I pray for myself and my children. It's from Ephesians 3:14b-21:

For this reason I kneel before the Father, from whom every family on earth derives its name. I pray that out of His glorious riches He may strengthen you with power through His Spirit in your inner being, so that Christ may dwell in your hearts through faith. And I pray that you, being rooted and established in love, may have power, together with all the Lord's holy people, to grasp how wide and long and high and deep is the love of Christ, and to know this love that surpasses all knowledge—that you may be filled to the measure of all the fullness of God.

Now to Him who is able to do immeasurably more than we ask or imagine, according to His power at work within us, to Him be glory in the church and in Christ Jesus throughout all generations, forever and ever! Amen (NIV).[55]

Does your inner-being need strengthened through the power of the Holy Spirit? You'll need it to live in your strengths, and let go of

---

55 New International Version, biblegateway.com

lesser-strengths. Do you need to be rooted and established in love? Do you need power to grasp how wide, how long, how high and deep is Jesus' love for you and your children?

I do.

I also need to be reminded that God is able to do immeasurably more than I can ask or imagine according to His power at work within me, for His honor and glory.

Sometimes when I don't know how to pray, I simply pray, "Lord, will you do immeasurably more than I can ask or imagine?"

He is faithful to do so.

Prayers of Release

Intimate prayer over your child allows God to bear fruit when you release them to His plan and future. Releasing a child doesn't happen on graduation day—it starts the moment they're born. Balancing right priorities keeps the end goals of parenting in sight, rather than surviving in the moment. Developing an intimacy with Jesus, through prayer, prepares you to release your children at the appropriate times.

Releasing your child into their future requires trusting God above a mother's instincts. It requires faith in God's character, His goodness, and sovereignty for the unknown of their futures.

It's a scary thing.

I thought I trusted God with my kids through their formative years. But when my oldest child was interested in a college eleven hours away, I failed to consider it might be God's plan for her. He spoke to me about *His* plan for her through a life-changing conversation in my living room.

Prayer isn't always a one-way conversation with God. It also includes conversations between the Holy Spirit and our spirit.

This prayer-conversation happened when I was listening to a Christian radio program during my daughter's senior year. I was thinking about her college choices when I heard the Holy Spirit say, "You aren't letting her choose." The following inaudible conversation between me and God transpired:

"She doesn't know what's best for her." I said.

"Don't you trust Me?"

"Of course I do, but she might make a choice you don't want her to make, one that draws her away from You."

"Don't you trust Me with what I want to do in her life?"

"Yes, but that's when she's on her own, when I'm not influential in her decisions anymore."

"I want to work in her life, but you're interfering."

"What?"

"I'm working in her life, but you're interfering. Get out of the way."

"Get out of the way? But she could do something really foolish."

"I know. Let her choose Me."

"What?"

"You have to release her to me."

"But it's hard. What if...?"

"Loosen your fingers and let Me work."

"I'm not ready."

"I know, but you're in the way if you stay where you are."

"It's not easy."

"I know. Do you trust Me?"

"Yes, but..."

"Do you trust Me?"

"Yes, Lord, but I'm scared."

"I know. Will you trust me?"

"Yes, Lord, but it's hard."

I stood there in my living room, sobbing, realizing God loved my daughter even more than I did. He told me going to a college several hours away was a stepping stone for mission work He was calling her to in other countries.

I needed to get out of the way so He could work in her life.

When my daughter decided to attend that university, so far away from our home, I trusted God with the unknowns of her future. Every fear a mother has materialized when we dropped her off in a place where she knew no one. I had to simply believe what God said was true—that He was working in her life, and I had to get out of the way.

Her experience at that university was life-changing. It was where she heard God's call for full-time mission work, where she made several trips to an orphanage in Guatemala.

If you want to hear God's perspective about your children, their faith, and their future, you have to develop an ear that's tuned to His voice, not to the world's noise around you. In John 10:27(NIV),[56] Jesus says, "My sheep listen to my voice; I know them, and they follow Me." As you develop an intimacy with Christ through reading His Word, being obedient, praying, and balancing priorities, hearing His voice will be easier.

Finally, A Mother's Prayer

I was reading a devotional one day when a piece of paper fell out of the book. I recognized the handwriting. It belonged to my mother-in-law, Lois. She was my mentor and the example of a godly woman. I opened up the paper. On it was written:

My Daily Prayer
If I can do some good today,
If I can serve along life's way,
If something helpful I can say,
Lord, show me how.
If I can right a human wrong,
If I can help to make one strong,
If I can cheer with smile or song,

---

56 New International Version, biblegateway.com

Lord, show me how.
If I can aid one in distress,
If I can make a burden less,
If I can spread more happiness,
Lord, show me how.[57]

My mother-in-law lived this prayer with humility and inspiration as a wife, mother, and friend. She came alongside me when I was a young mom and gently modeled biblical motherhood. Not only that, she poured her life into people around her. When you were with her, you felt as though time stopped. You felt you were the only person on the earth who mattered, even though her life was busy.

She lived moments with God's grace. When she unexpectedly died at sixty-seven, she left this world with no regrets. It's the legacy she left behind. That's the simplest summary of balanced living I can offer.

This prayer reminds me that the most important things we do in life are what we do when no one's looking. It's living well because we only have one life to live.

I don't know whether my mother-in-law prayed this prayer daily. All I know is that she lived it.

"Help me be kind, Lord, show me the way."

That's how I want to live. It's how I want my children to remember me.

How about you?

---

57 Author Unknown

Reflection
Where do you need to develop an intimacy with Christ?

What areas do you need to give up control, allowing God to draw your child to Him?

How can you develop an ear to hear God's voice?

Dear Father, will You show me how to be kind today? Please show me how to be kind to my kids when my patience is short. Teach me to be kind to my husband when I'm disappointed. Help me to pare down what I expect of myself and be wise with my time. Give me grace to be patient with those I'm with today. Help me to live life well. Lord, show me the way.

Come Unto Me

*"Come to me, all you who are weary and
burdened, and I will give you rest."*

MATTHEW 11:28, NIV[58]

If you've come to the end of this book realizing you don't really
know Jesus, the Son of God, you can begin a personal relationship
with Him right now. He loves you and desires to have a relationship
with you.

First, do you know that all of us are sinners? "For all have sinned
and fall short of the glory of God" (Romans 3:23, NIV).[59]

Because of our sin, we are separated from God because He is holy.
Our sin results in spiritual and eternal death. "For the wages of sin
is death, but the gift of God is eternal life in Jesus Christ our Lord"
(Romans 6:23, NIV).[60]

But God loves you and I so much that He sent His son, Jesus Christ,
to die on the cross, bearing the weight of our sin, so we could have eternal life in heaven. "But God demonstrates His own love for us in this:
While we were still sinners, Christ died for us" (Romans 5:8, NIV).[61]

---

58 New International Version, biblegateway

59 New International Version, biblegateway.com

60 New International Version, biblegateway.com

61 New International Version, biblegateway.com

Not only did Jesus die on the Cross, but He rose from the dead on the third day and ascended into heaven where He now resides with God. Because of His victory over death, we, too, have victory over death when we receive Jesus Christ as our Savior. This gift of eternal life isn't from anything we can earn, it's a free gift from God.

"For it is by grace you have been saved, through faith—and this is not from yourselves, it is the gift of God, not by words, so that no one can boast" Ephesians 2:8-9, NIV.[62]

To receive this free gift of eternal life in heaven and an abundant life on earth, you simply need to confess that Jesus is the Son of God, ask Him to forgive your sins, and receive His death as payment for your salvation. When you do this, He comes to live in you through His Holy Spirit.

"If you declare with your mouth, 'Jesus is Lord,' and believe in your heart that God raised Him from the dead, you will be saved. For it is with your heart that you believe and are justified, and it is with your mouth that you profess your faith and are saved" Romans 10:9-10 (NIV).[63]

You can receive Jesus as your Savior right now by praying this prayer or a similar one;

Jesus, I confess that I'm a sinner. I believe you are the Son of God, that you died on the Cross to bear my sins, and You rose from the dead three days later. I receive your forgiveness as payment for my sins. Come and live in my heart so I can have eternal life with You in heaven and an abundant life here on earth. Thank you for loving me and for being my Lord and Savior. Amen.

---

62 New International Version, biblegateway.com
63 New International Version, biblegateway.com

That's it! You are now a daughter of the King of Kings! Receive His grace and practice the principles we've talked about in developing a relationship with Jesus. You are loved.

If you've prayed this prayer and started a new relationship with Jesus Christ, I'd love to hear from you! Email me at yoderbl@gmail.com.

About the Author

Brenda L. Yoder is a national speaker, free-lance writer, counselor, and teacher. She has a Master's Degree in Clinical Mental Health Counseling, and a B.A. in Education. After being a stay-at-home-mom and high school teacher, she's currently a school counselor with a private counseling and coaching practice. She received the "Powerful Connection" award for teachers in 2003 & 2004. She's also a  parenting columnist for several online magazines, and has a mental health column in her hometown paper.

Brenda has been featured in *Chicken Soup for the Soul: Reboot Your Life* and has co-authored curriculums on teen dating violence and foster care parenting. Her newest resource for teen girls, "*Who Do You Say I Am?*" can be found at her website, brendayoder.com.

Brenda's a popular speaker for women's retreats, youth conferences, seminars, MOPS groups, and church events. You can connect with Brenda's ministry, *Life Beyond The Picket Fence*, at brendayoder.com, where she writes about life, faith, and parenting beyond the storybook image.

If you'd like Brenda to bring the *Balance, Busyness and Not Doing It All* retreat to your area or women's group, contact Brenda at yoderbl@gmail.com.

Brenda and her husband have four children who range in age from teens to early twenties. They live on a farm in northern Indiana. Connect with Brenda on Twitter, Facebook, Pinterest, or at brendayoder.com.